SARDIN[

DIVING GUIDE

SWAN·HILL

PRESS

SARDINIA
DIVING GUIDE

Texts and photographs
Egidio Trainito

Illustrations and maps
Stefano Trainito

Editorial Coordination
Valeria Manferto De Fabianis

Graphic design
Patrizia Balocco Lovisetti
Clara Zanotti

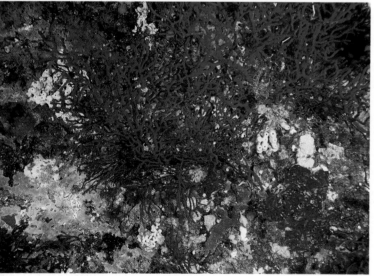

1 A carpet of jewel anemones (Corynactis viridis) covers the rock on the walls north of Secca di Su Puntillone . This is one of the most interesting natural sights in the waters of Sardinia.

2-3 Gorgonians, alcyonarians and golden zoanthids compete for space on the rocks of Secca del Papa.

4 top The camera flash reveals the bright colors of a red scorpionfish.

4 bottom Animals dominate in poorly illuminated areas: hundreds of organisms, sponges and gorgonians crowded on top of each other cover the wall at Secca Washington.

Contents

The author would like to thank:
Fulvio and Lodovica Poncini - Nautilus - Palau; Renato Romor and Giovanni Pinto - Centro Immersioni Figarolo - Golfo Aranci; Cinzia, Roberta Calamita and Maurizio Uras - L'Argonauta - Cala Gonone; Marco Puggioni and Marco Foddis - Nautica Centro Sub - S.Maria Navarrese; Vincenzo Sicbaldi - Airsub Service - Cagliari; Andrea and Milena Vadilonga - Cagliari; Gianluigi Angius and Stefano Masala- Cagliari; Ornella Girosi and Gepi Caria - Carloforte Tonnara and Isla Diving Center - Carloforte; Giuseppe and Mariangela Cappai + 1 - Malu Entu Diving - S'Archittu; Vincenzo Piras - Bosa Diving Center ; Antonio Achilli and Alessandro Sirigu - Associazione Aquamarina Sassari; Alessandro "Popi" Valoncini and Giovanni Messina- Diving Center Costa Paradiso; Mario, Lalla, Pina, Monica, Claudio, Enrico, Simona, Clara, Sara, Franca del Centro Sub Tavolara and all those who put up with me and supported me during this work.

© 1997 White Star S.r.l.
First Published in the UK in 1997 by Swan Hill Press, an imprint of Airlife Publishing Ltd.

British Library Cataloguing in Publication Data
A catalogue record for this book is available from the British Library
ISBN 1-85310-922-3

Printed in Italy by Grafedit, (Bergamo).
in the month of May 1997
Colour separations by Fotomec, (Torino).

SWAN HILL PRESS
an imprint of Airlife Publishing Ltd.
101 Longden Road,
Shrewsbury SY3 9EB, England

STRAIT OF BONIFACIO

MADDALENA ISLAND
CAPRERA ISLAND
27
28
26
PALAU
29
Mortorio island
ASINARA ISLAND
25
30
GULF OF OLBIA
GULF OF ASINARA
2
1
Capo Figari
Capo Falcone
4
3
Tavolara island
OLBIA
5
6
7
Molara island

MAR DI SARDEGNA

SASSARI

Capo Comino

24
ALGHERO
Capo Caccia

OROSEI
8
23
BOSA
9
CALA GONONE
22
GULF OF OROSEI
10
11
21
12
Capo Mannu
Capo di Mt. Santu

13
ORISTANO
ARBATAX
Capo Bellavista

GULF OF ORISTANO

Capo della Frasca

Capo Pecora

Capo Ferrato

GULF OF GONNESA
20
CAGLIARI
S. Pietro island
VILLASIMIUS
19
16
S.Antioco island
15
GULF OF
14
CAGLIARI
18

TYRRHENIAN SEA

17
Capo
Teulada
Capo
Spartivento

INTRODUCTION

The fragrance of strawflowers, broom, rosemary and hundreds of other plants is the first thing you'll notice about the coast of Sardinia, even before your gaze wanders to the reefs and the long tongues of sand, and before your eyes are indelibly impressed with the dark blue to turquoise palette of colors that is the sea of Sardinia. It cannot be compared with any other tropical sea - there is something unique about it. Perhaps it is the transparent water, or perhaps the landscape in general. Another

A

sensation, not as immediate but just as strong, grows gradually as you sail along the coast of the island, and continues even when you dive underwater. It is the sign of passing time, of the enormous masses of water that have lapped, submerged and revealed the rocks and the sand that surround the island. It may seem a strange play on words, but the ancient name for Sardinia, Ichnusa, means "imprint," and the perimeter of the island does indeed show the indelible imprint of time. There are evident signs of the sea level pulsating against stable land where volcanic tumult ended far back in geological time. Thus, above

water, on the limestone cliffs soaring 8 to 11 meters over the sea, the furrow carved by the waves 120,000 years ago is perfectly visible. And underwater, from quite shallow depths down to 60 meters deep, long ribbons of fossil beach are mute testimony
to the slow rising of the sea level, which about 20,000 years ago was 120 meters below the current level. Geologists call them beach rocks, while Sardinians more colorfully and creatively refer to them as Roman roads, granites or brinks. Parallel to the present-day coastline are groups of conglomerate masses, a cracked and fissured mixture of sandstone and pebbles with generally only a few points resting

B

on the seabed, thus forming deep clefts. Like a dotted line that follows the entire perimeter of the island both above and below sea level, these signs of passing time seem proof that the boundary between land and sea is ephemeral, not only because it changes over time, but also and perhaps especially because underwater the landscape of the coast seems to continue unbroken. These underwater scenes, so impossible to capture by the limited technology of photography, remain indelibly imprinted in the memory of anyone who dives here, even more than the innumerable forms of life that cover them and swim around them.

Sardinia in the Mediterranean

Although the Mediterranean Sea is substantially homogenous from the biogeographical perspective, that is in the distribution of its forms of life, it is commonly divided into several distinct areas. To the west, the Alboran Sea, from the island of the same name located south of Spain, marks the boundary of and point of exchange with the Atlantic Ocean.
The western Mediterranean includes the central area from the Balearic Islands to Sicily. The Adriatic and the eastern Mediterranean are the other two areas that mark the northeastern portion and far eastern edge of the basin. Sardinia is right in the middle of the central Mediterranean, in a position which is universally considered conducive to creating a synthesis of the biological characteristics of the entire area. The origins of the species which now populate the Mediterranean can be traced back to the period in which all the continents on the Earth were part of a single enormous supercontinent called Pangea, into which flowed a deep gulf, the Tetide Sea. The Tetide Sea, located more or less where the Mediterranean is today, is considered the Mediterranean's area of origin.
It was a warm sea populated by large numbers of tropical species. Around that time, about 210 million years ago, the phenomenon of continental drift began: the great clumps of the earth's crust which are the present-day continents began to move, breaking the unity of Pangea and creating new seas. It required about two hundred million more years of continental drift to shape the Mediterranean into something akin to its present form. Around the end of this period, between 25 and 16 million years ago, the mass which now constitutes Sardinia and Corsica, almost a

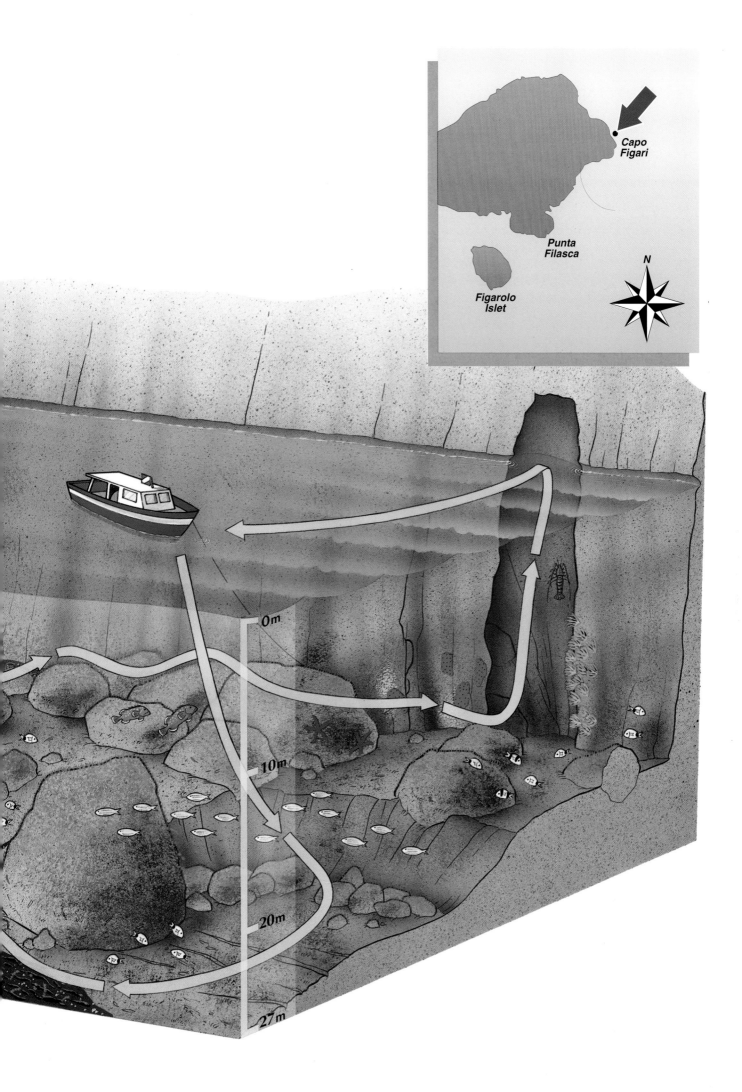

Capo Figari

Punta Filasca

Figarolo Islet

N

0m

10m

20m

27m

A - The promontory of Capo Figari closes off the great Gulf of Olbia to the north. It is a piece of the limestone sheath that continues south from the island of Tavolara to the Gulf of Orosei. The cape slopes down toward the interior, while it juts out to sea with vertical walls.

Passing the tip of Capo Figari heading north, you come to a ledge in the wall facing the northeast. It is called Mamuthone due to the similarity of its profile with the Carnival mask of the same name from the city of Momoiada, in the Nuoro area. A little farther north the wall above the water has a large cavity called the Grotta Nera (Black Grotto). Anchor close to the wall over a mixed rock and detrital seabed about 24 meters deep. Descend along the mooring line and immediately head south.
The seabed slopes down gently to 27 meters deep, with coralligenous formations that cover low rocks. From here a slope of coral with

D

B - Under the cliffs of the cape, the underwater environment shows the effects of reduced sunlight, and plants and animals typical of less illuminated areas predominate. A large red star (Ophidiaster ophidianus) with its gaudy purple color crawls through the algae.

C - Spiny lobsters, which are nocturnal creatures, live in the fissures between the rocks, even at shallow depths. They are generally small in size, as the larger ones now remain at great depths to avoid continuous fishing.

A

B

C

E

D - At the foot of the cliff, a projection forms crevices colonized by various organisms, especially animals. Sponges, cnidarians and bryozoans grow on a substratum of calcareous red algae. The low light creates habitats typical of deeper waters.

E - Yellow sea fans (Eunicella cavolinii) are typical of precoralligenous zones at the base of the cliffs of Capo Figari. The position of the fan indicates the presence of currents around the base of the wall.

F - Numerous cowries (Luria lurida) live in the dark caves and crevices. This mollusk covers its entire shell with its mantle, becoming quite mimetic. This cover is what makes its shell as bright as porcelain.

a jagged edge broken by fractures and gullies descends to a detrital seabed 35 meters deep. The more classic route continues among an accumulation of large rocky masses at 27 meters bathymetric line.
On the rocks there are bryozoans and small colonies of Parerythopodium. A large flat mass resting on the others forms a vault about 1 meter high, carpeted by stony corals (Leptosammia pruvoti). Several large brown meagres also swim in the dark: if you approach them carefully you will be able to observe them quite closely, keeping your flashlight off until the last minute. The meagres will retreat a bit as the light shines on them, but not enough to be out of sight.

Around you, in the crevices and holes among the masses, numerous schools of anthias swim, each with its dominant male, larger and more colorful than the females.

Then ascend among the reefs where you can see a beautiful grouper, a conger eel, and swimming in the distant ocean depths, schools of seabreams and salemas. On the flat areas among the rocks you will see lairs of large octopuses, which are quite visible due to the accumulation of rocks and shells that marks the entries. Then ascend to the base of the rocky wall, where at about one meter from the seabed there is a horizontal ledge that follows the pattern of the cliffs. In the shadow of this canopy there is an environment typical of poorly illuminated areas, with golden zoanthids, bryozoans, annelids and sea fans that grow on a carpet of red algae. Follow the base of the wall and turn north to see another accumulation of masses where two beautiful groupers are hiding, not particularly intimidated by the approach of divers. Among the algae on the higher part of the masses a large red star (*Ophidiaster ophidianus*) is passing through, and all around swim lovely schools of salemas. Continue until you come to the masses located at the bottom of a wide crack 18 meters deep. This is an open cave that comes out of the water at a pronounced vertical angle and enters the wall in a V form. Right at the entry you can see a nice

I

J

G - Large red scorpionfish (Scorpaena scrofa) are common among the rocky masses on the seabed. Scorpionfish are predators that use mimicry and speed to capture their prey.

H - A conger eel (Conger conger) hides among the rocks, covered by large patches of encrusting sponges. The conger eel is a nocturnal predator with an elongated body. During the day it lives in lairs.

I - Brown meagres (Sciaena umbra) are quite common in the caves and crevices of Capo Figari. They often gather in dense schools at the entrances to their lairs, ready to retreat at the first sign of disturbance.

J - Octopuses, which may become quite large, are also quite common among the rockslides of the cape. Predators by night, by day octopuses tend to live in lairs, at the entrances to which they pile pebbles and shells which they use to block the entry.

F

G

H

group of brown meagres. Then enter the crack and go about 30 meters; the view toward the outside is quite lovely. Ascend up the walls of the cave with a first jump at 15 meters deep and a second at 3 meters. On the walls there is a classic succession of dark areas, where the golden zoanthids are gradually replaced by *Leptosammia cnidarians* until, in the more interior part, the presence of animals attached to the walls drops drastically. In the darker areas you can see cowries, lobsters and squills, while near the surface, where the hydrodynamics increase, the rock is covered with thick colonies of hydrozoans. After an entertaining safety stop which you can pass watching the small organisms that cover the rock, you'll surface over the deepest area of the crack, which exits on the outside and, after an initial portion with a low pyramid-shaped vault, turns into a broad opening where a rock arch separates the main entrance from a passage hole about 10 meters from the surface. The plays of light and shadow on the emerging rocks are quite beautiful, while the water is a deep turquoise blue. Come out of the cave and you'll be just a few meters from the boat moored right in front of you.

TEDJA LISCIA

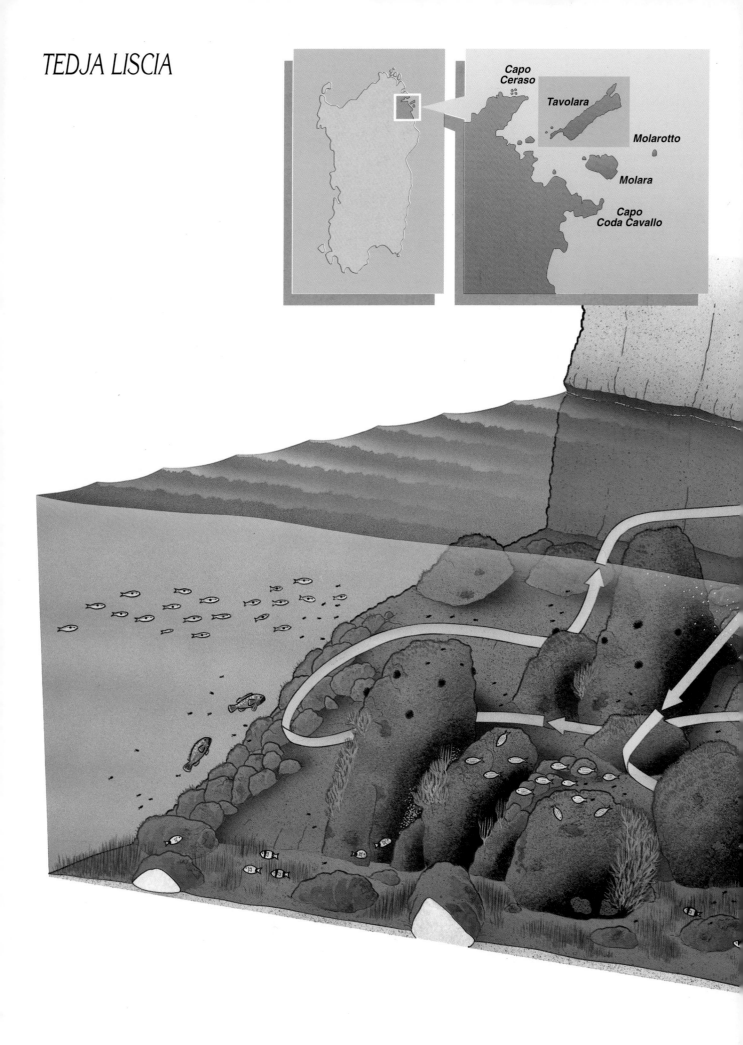

Capo
Ceraso

Tavolara

Molarotto

Molara

Capo
Coda Cavallo

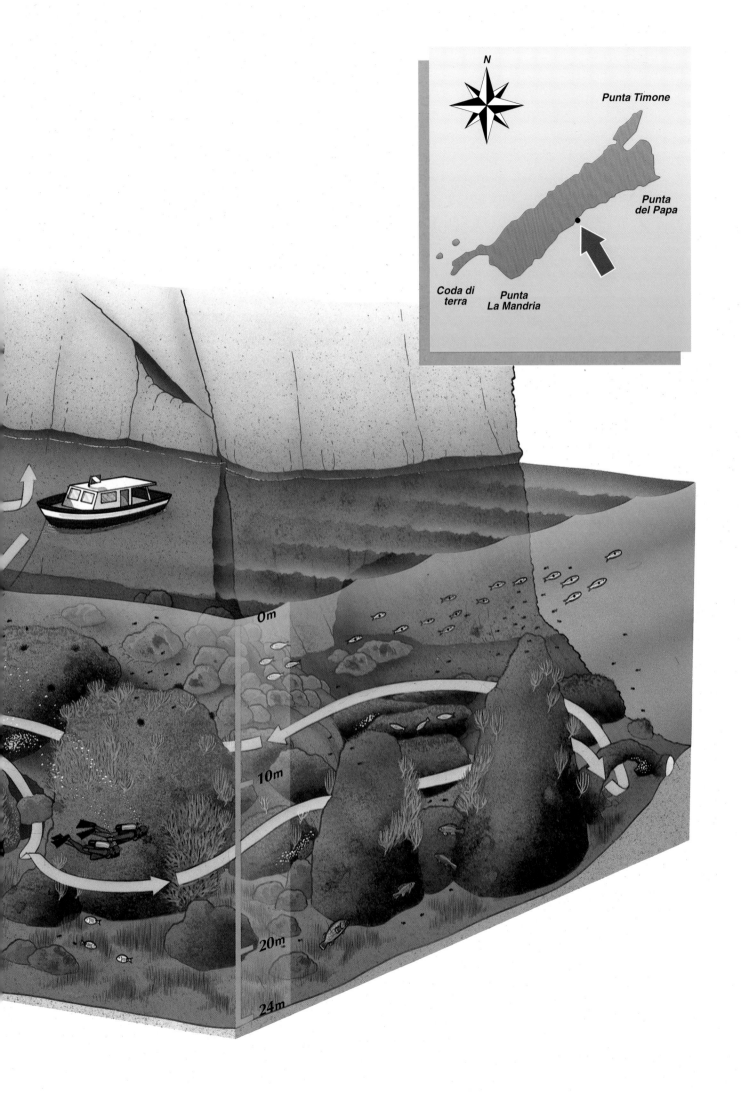

Punta Timone

Punta del Papa

Coda di terra

Punta La Mandria

0m

10m

20m

24m

A - Molarotto is a rock surrounded by numerous shallows that continue the forms of the emerged rocks underwater, with rocky bastions separated by channels.

B - The rocks of the northeast shallow are covered with a thin layer of algae, due to the effects of hydrodynamics and the work of grazing fish and invertebrates.

C - The base of the rocks is often colonized by yellow gorgonians and orange sponges, a sign that the sea carries in nutrition to these invertebrates even near the sea floor.

D - The Molarotto landscape is distinguished by the presence of rocky projections rising up vertically.

E - The water at Molarotto is always crystal clear, and abundant light penetrates, making the scene even more fascinating.

F - Morays, sometimes in groups of two or three in the same lair, are common among the masses on the seabed. They can often be seen even during the day as they slither out in the open among the rocks.

G - The upper portions of the shallow are always surrounded by a dense cloud of damselfish.

H - Large red scorpionfish are common on the deeper rocks of the shallow.

G - A blenny hovers among the algae that cover the shallower rocks. Blennies prey on small invertebrates, which they capture with swift movements; in fact, their bodies are designed to dart forward rapidly and not to swim long distances.

dive. As you swim among the masses, morays seem to be everywhere: large specimens peep out of almost every fissure, sometimes two or three of them at once. It is not uncommon to see them swimming quite far from the rocks, ready to take cover if divers approach. You will also see large red scorpionfish which are not easy to spot due to their remarkable mimetic abilities. The rock bastions toward the open sea terminate almost vertically, forming walls which on their northern sides are covered with red sponges and golden zoanthids. Like the granite of the emerging reef, underwater as well the rocks are furrowed by deep fissures, *tafoni* and passage holes,

E

and create quite a lovely scene. In the fissures hide large groupers which can often be seen out in the open, head down. The shallow has special attractions. You may see an enormous ray, sometimes poised on the patches of detritus on the seabed and sometimes on a flat rock. The summer spectacle is a large school of Mediterranean barracudas patrolling the shallow. But above all, as you swim upward on the return trip, it is possible to see large pelagic fish, including amberjacks, dentex, and even swordfish. Yet one of the most beautiful spectacles on this shallow, as you ascend, is the enormous cloud of damselfish that rhythmically drifts above the spires of the rocks illuminated by the sun.

F

G

H

I

THE WRECK OF MOLARA

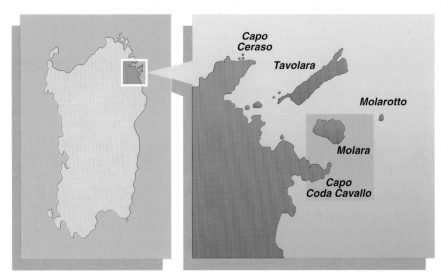

Capo Ceraso
Tavolara
Molarotto
Molara
Capo Coda Cavallo

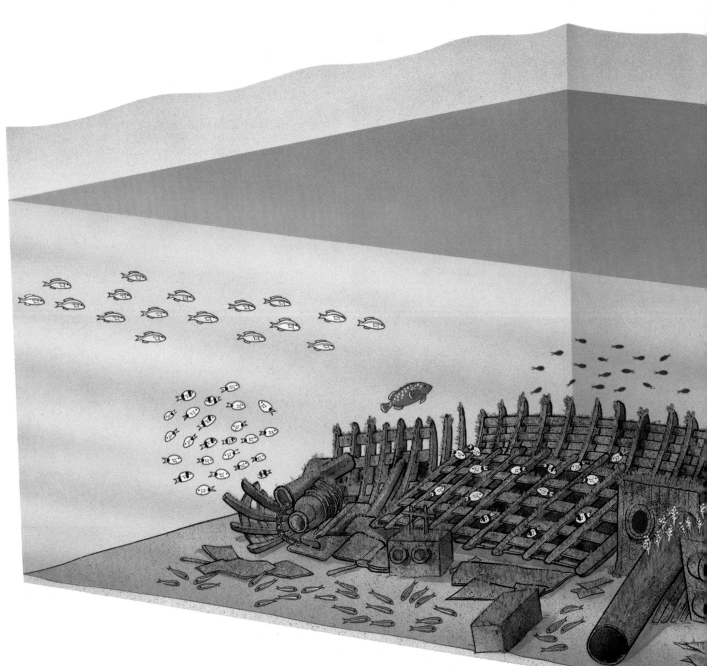

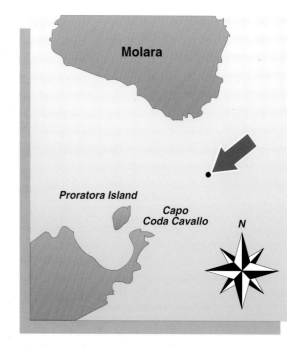

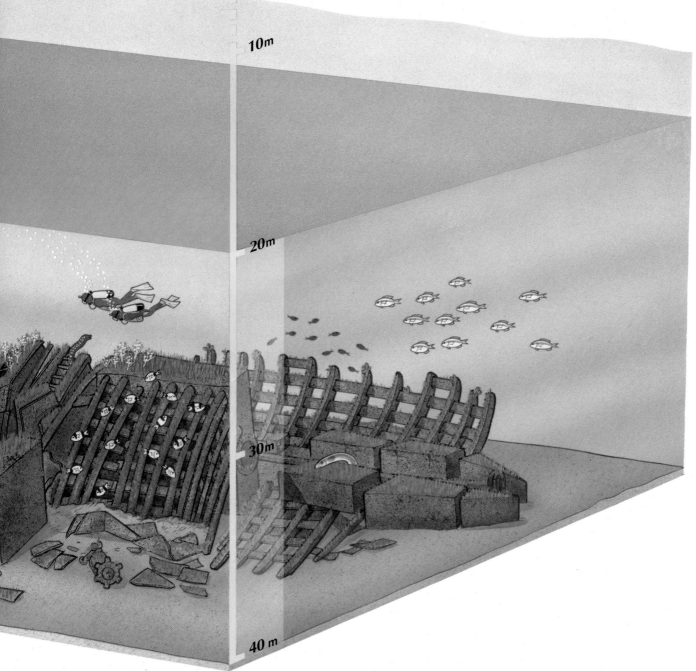

Between Molara and Capo Coda Cavallo on a sandy seabed 39 meters deep lies the large hulk of a wreck which until recently was largely still a mystery. For a long time it was thought to be an armed cargo ship transporting provisions that was torpedoed by a British submarine, as was the case of many other wrecks along the Sardinian coast. There are witnesses to such an event who recount how the ship caught fire before sinking. Yet many clues seem to indicate that the ship referred to in these tales was another one that appears to be lying on the sea floor not far from the Molara wreck. This ship is indeed quite damaged and shows clear signs of a fire. Not only does the Molara wreck show no sign of fire, but above all the type of construction and the age of the ship seem to place it well before 1943. Recent research and a new eyewitness to the events now give us a rather clear picture of what happened during the early months of 1943. Outside of Capo Coda Cavallo in the early spring of that year,

B - The wreck of Molara was a three-mast ship built in the second half of the 19th century. The photo shows the support of the stern mast, which is lying in the sand on the left side of the wreck.

C - The wreck had few structures on the deck: in addition to the masts in the stern area there were the smokestacks, which have now been destroyed.

D - The ship was a mixed iron and wood construction. Only a few fragments remain of the wooden portions, while the iron frame is well-preserved. Many organisms, especially lilac sponges (Haliclona mediterranea), have colonized the higher structures.

A - During World War Two the Italian and German convoys that sailed along the eastern coast of Sardinia were subject to continuous, damaging attacks by English submarines. In 1943, two ships were sunk not far from Capo Coda Cavallo: a minesweeper and the Molara wreck.

English submarines sank at least two ships, a mine-sweeper and old, creaky steamboat which was transporting bales of tobacco and probably grain. While the first has not yet been found, it is probably the "armed cargo ship" of which there has been so much talk, while the second is probably our wreck. It is a large ship of mixed wood and steel construction, over 70 meters long and in all likelihood with a gross tonnage of over 2,000. It was a motor sailer, or a ship with mixed propulsion, both sail and steam - this is quite clear from the great two-piston steam engine and the support structures of the two masts clearly visible on the wreck. These two clues decisively date the construction of the ship to the end of the 19th century, placing it in that brief transitory phase in the history of naval construction that led to the disappearance of large sailing ships and the definitive victory of motor navigation, which was safer and faster. When it was sunk it was already almost an antique. Probably of French origin, it was headed for Marseilles from Syria. In addition to its French captain, it had a crew of

12-13 black seamen. It was torpedoed in the open sea by a British submarine. Only its captain was captured, while its crew, which had taken refuge on a lifeboat, was released. With this explanation of its history and the reason for its sinking, the Molara wreck is above all a piece of industrial archeology of great historical interest that adds further charm to the dive. Enter the water, and at a depth of about 20 meters the dark shape of the wreck begins to materialize on the faint light of the seabed. The highest portions at a depth of 35 meters consist of the large section that contained the enormous steam engine, the smokebox and the boiler. The smokestack has fallen toward the left side and the end is resting on the sand. The ship appears dismembered, and it takes some time to determine the position of the hull and identify the various pieces piled on top of each other, because little remains of the planking and the other wooden coverings. Along the steel frames around the joint nails only a few fragments of wood remain, which have resisted only because they are permeated with iron oxide. The double T-shaped large beam of the keelson which, given its position, shows that the hull is resting on its left side and that the right side has collapsed, falling on top of it, is clearly visible. Given the depth, it is not possible to visit the whole wreck in a single dive, and thus you should concentrate on the aft side and the steam engine. From the engine area move to the right side of the hull where the structures of the frame poke out from the sand, looking like the rib cage of a large whale. The ends of the frame are covered by violet-colored tubular sponges that stand out in your flashlight beam on the rusted iron. Moving toward the stern, you will come to the end of the large transmission shaft with its various flange joints. Around the axle are scattered tank caissons, formed to fit the hull as it narrowed. There is no trace of the propeller. Coming back toward the engine, the tangle of structures becomes chaotic. The upper part of the right side has collapsed on the left, and in the

F

G

E

H

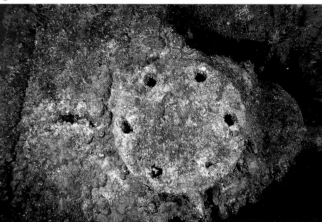

E - The iron beam of the keelson runs through the central portion of the hull. On it are the flanges that supported the bearings of the propeller axle.

F - The steam engine is lying on its side, and among the pipes and iron fragments there are several gauges which have lost their glass faces, but not their pointers.

G - The motor had two cylinders and three columns. The enormous attachment flange of the propeller axle is clearly visible.

H - Schools of seabreams, numerous morays, conger eels and large groupers hide among the remains of the hull.

middle swim numerous two-banded seabreams, many of which are enormous for this species. You then come to the engine. It is a double effect steam engine with two cylinders and three support columns. The connecting flange of the axle and a group of gauges that still have their pointers are quite visible on the motor. Enormous seabreams also swim inside the engine. Among the

scrap iron hide a large moray and big groupers, which are quite timid even though they often hide just below the tallest pieces of wreckage. Colonies of hydrozoans grow on the higher portions, often grazed by brightly colored nudibranch gastropods (*Flabellina ischitana*), while tall fronds of sargassum are supported by aerocysts.
Under the engine is a pile of bricks

which made up the refractory covering of the boiler, which is right under the large smokestacks. Until recently a conger eel known as Willie lived here. Accustomed to divers, Willie would rub up against them in exchange for a small fish. He is now gone, because someone with tanks dove all the way down here to shoot him, an act which was as stupid as it was illegal.
The mouths of the smokestacks have been colonized by brightly colored sea anemones that take advantage of the channeling effect of the currents passing through the large tubes. This classical wreck dive ends here, and as you ascend you will see piles of materials along the left side: caissons, cables and various fragments. You can see the two windlasses near the bow, which has split open like a walnut, with a nice school of seabreams swimming over it. Often, at the limits of visibility, you may see large dentex sailing by, and thus, as you rise to the surface, your sensation of having only glimpsed the secret of this wreck is compounded by the mysterious fascination of the great pelagic fish.

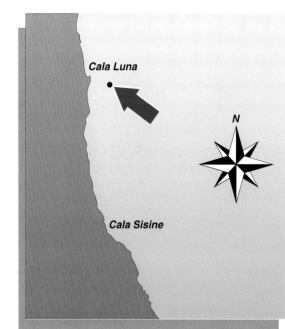

Cala Luna

Cala Sisine

N

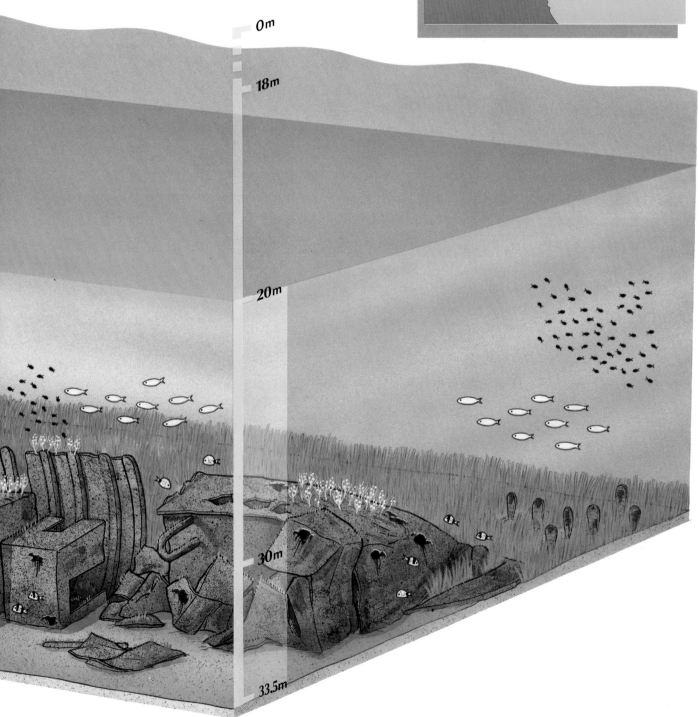

0m

18m

20m

30m

33.5m

A - Cala Luna

B

C

D

A cross from Cala Luna, about a half a mile out to sea on a mixed seabed of detritus and Neptune grass, lies the wreck of the *Nasello*. Built in Hamburg in 1921, it was an auxiliary, type F67 ship, and on April 3, 1943 it was transporting munitions for German troops.
Like the *KT* in the Gulf of Orosei, the Nasello was also hit by artillery from the Allied submarine Safari as it sailed across from Cala Gonone.
On that same day, the deadly British submarine, which in 1943 was patrolling the eastern coast of Sardinia, also sank the S. Francesco di Paola,

E

a 77 ton motor sailer, across from nearby Cala Sisine.
The *Nasello*, its center ripped by grenades, went adrift in the gulf before exploding and sinking.
The wreck, which was originally 42 meters long and 7.5 meters wide, is resting on its left side, and the devastated central area is standing up on end, unlike the stern and aft.
When you come to the stern, you will immediately see the large rudder lying on the seabed, and only one blade of the propeller sticks out of the sand.
Swim above the right broadside toward the deck, part of which is pulled out and reduced to contorted wreckage.

A - Cala Luna has become one of the classic summer holiday areas in Sardinia. Few know that on a fateful morning in 1943, two ships were sunk off this beautiful beach by the English submarine the Safari.

B - The bow of the Nasello is resting on its left side: the ship was shattered by explosions and has shattered into three pieces. A fairlead on the front of the bow was probably used to pull the ship.

C - A large windlass is clearly visible among the deck structures, with its steel cable still wound around the central coil.

D - The ship sank after it was hit by a torpedo that exploded the cargo of explosives it was transporting. Many structures were ripped out and lie piled on top of each other.

F

G - The small cabin in the center of the wreck is lying on its left side, while the upper portion is surrounded by a guardrail. All around there are piles of wreckage which are hard to identify.

H - Schools of seabreams and a pair of groupers can often be seen around the central portion of the wreck. One of the two groupers is extremely large.

I - In the stern, the rudder is lying on the sand, while one blade of the propeller is poking out of the sediment. Even at this depth the currents carry in sand and have slowly covered several structures.

Proceed along what remains of the deck structures toward the bow, and you will come to two rooms on the left side.

The first is smaller and its walls are mostly missing, while the larger second one must have been the higher part of the ship, with a guardrail along its upper perimeter.

The central area is a mass of wreckage which is not easy to identify. You can clearly see a large windlass with its steel cable still wound.

At least a portion of the right broadside seems to be standing. Here in the tangle of cables, iron slabs, pipes and plate live a pair of groupers.

One, a female, is small, while the other is a large male which weighs at least 20 kilograms. Sargassum grows on the raised portions; it is easily identifiable by its erect posture and the spherical cysts that grow at the base of the lance-shaped fronds.

The bow is at the end of the area hit by the explosion.

Lying on its left side, it seems practically intact: a guardrail follows its profile and on the small deck portion remaining there are several hatches, from one of which peeps the head of a beautiful conger eel.

At the end of the bow an anchor winch pulley is still in place, and the two anchors poke out of the hawseholes.

These are two Hall anchors weighing about 200 kilos each: the one on the left is clearly visible on the broadside, and as it is protruding it is kept clean by the current.

The one on the right is below the bow, but fully visible.

From the bow return toward the anchor, reaching a shallower depth in order to get a view of the entire hull.

When there is some current and visibility is good, an overall view of the hull not only gives you a better idea of the structure of the ship, but in particular shows you quite clearly the violence of the explosions that first ripped apart and then sank the *Nasello*.

G

H

E - The bow, still almost completely intact, is quite impressive. The anchors are still poking out of the hawseholes: the one on the right is clearly visible.

F - The right anchor, a Hall, has been kept clean by the currents. The left anchor can be seen under the bow.

I

THE SOUTHERN COAST: FROM ARBATAX TO BOSA

Capo di Monte Santu closes off the Gulf of Orosei from the south. This cape has a low outline with vegetation growing thickly down to the edge of the wall. Leave the vertiginous walls of the gulf behind you and descend south, passing the Pedra Longa spire where the calcareous landscape ends. From the little island of Ogliastra at the center of the Gulf of Tortolì to Capo Sferracavallo, the granite returns

Corona Niedda
Su Puntillone
S'Archittu
●ORISTANO
GULF OF ORISTANO
Le Tacche Bianche
Scoglio del Corno
SAN PIETRO ISLAND
SAN ANTIOCO ISLAND
Banco Pomata
Scoglio del Toro
GULF OF OROSEI
Acituan Caves
Secca dell'Isolotto
CAGLIARI
The Wreck of the Entella
The Wreck of the Romagna
Secca di Mezzo
GULF OF CAGLIARI

A - The small Oasis of Torre Seu in Sinis is a protected area managed by the WWF, and until La Maddalena Archipelago National Park was established it was the only coastal area of Sardinia which was protected.

B - The coast between Nebida and Masua is one of the wildest areas of the island. In the background to the left are the vertical walls of the Pan di Zucchero reef: the rocks on this stretch of the coast are the most ancient of the entire continent of Europe.

with jagged spires and pinnacles. Farther south on the coastal stretch at Salto di Quirra to Capo S.Lorenzo, the limestone returns. The whole area has very interesting seabeds with faboulous caves: unfortunately, it is subject to military restrictions. After Capo S.Lorenzo the stretch of coast from the mouth of the Flumendosa to Capo Ferrato, south of Muravera, is low and delimited by sandbanks with large marshes behind them, including the Colostrai marsh. Across from Capo Ferrato, again formed by volcanic rock, is a beautiful shallow which is also known as Secca delle Cicale due to the large quantity of these crustaceans that gather among the rocks in late spring. During World War II at least two large cargo ships were sunk here, although they lie at practically inaccessible depths. A little farther south the granite coast of Villasimius begins, with the islands of Serpentara and Cavoli off the coast. Unfortunately the entire stretch of sea from Serpentara to Capo Boi is restricted to archeological excavations, and diving is forbidden. Only recently have a few diving centers obtained permission to dive in certain areas. This is one of the most interesting areas in Sardinia for diving, yet a short-sighted desire to protect archeological treasures has prevented its use. Moreover, the prohibition has in no way stopped

poachers, and the illegal removal of archeological finds continues despite prohibitions. Fortunately, beautiful dives are possible even outside the area, on the offshore shallows and on the wreck of the Egle, a cargo ship lying 36 meters deep which was sunk by a submarine. The wrecks are one of the characteristic features of the seabeds in the Gulf of Cagliari: there are at least fifteen of them, but only two can be explored without diving over 40 meters deep. Across from the promontory of Torre delle Stelle, in addition to the remains of the *Entella*, the remains of two other convoy ships sunk between April 10 and 11, 1943 lie at depths between 40 and 70 meters. The *Loredan*, a 1,350 ton ship, lies in the deepest water, and in addition to still having cannons and machine gun posts in place, its wreckage is covered with large fans of red and yellow gorgonians. Passing the Gulf of Cagliari, there is yet another wreck just before Capo Teulada, where the hull of the *Dino*, a mercantile ship that was transporting clay and sank in 1973 during a sea storm, lies in the harbor of Porto Zafferano at a depth of 25 meters. Unfortunately, the wreck lies within the prohibited military zone, and in fact near Capo Teulada is a military exercise area and firing ground for the Decimomannu air base. In theory, it is prohibited to dive here as well, but on Sunday and during the summer the military makes an exception, and a few quick dives onto the wreck are possible - the usual Italian-style solution. Doubling the ancient calcareous cliffs of Capo Teulada, the islets of Toro, Vacca and Vitello prepare you for the two islands of S. Antioco and Carloforte. The outer edges of both islands offer wild landscapes almost untouched by humans. Underwater, there are numerous beautiful diving areas, where the most interesting aspect is offered by the clear difference in animal and plant groups that populate the submerged rocks. Compared with the northern and eastern coasts, you will immediately notice the difference in the algae coverage, the almost total absence of gorgonians and, for example, the greater number of ornate wrasses rather than rainbow wrasses: the exact contrary from the opposite coast. From the reef of Carloforte, which consists of dramatic masses of volcanic rock, look east to see the calcareous coast of the larger island. This is one of the zones with which divers are less familiar, for reasons which include the fact that tourism, with its joys and pains, has only just begun here, but it is also the oldest stretch of coast on the entire continent of Europe. Between Nebida and Masua the limestone, which in many areas drops sheer to the sea, is over 500 million years old. Across from the larger island is Pan del Zucchero, a steep calcareous rock covered with low vegetation only on its highest part. Underwater along its walls the seabed does not reach great depths, and interesting cavities open up in the calcareous rock. The coast continues high until the deep inlet of Cala Domestica. Then, passing Buggerru, the great beach of Portixeddu leads north to Capo Pecora. This is the wildest part of the coast on the island, mostly inaccessible by land and still unexplored by divers. And here the sea, exposed as it is to the west, is no laughing matter. One must go much farther north, to the Oristano area, to find organized diving centers. But before arriving, you will see extraordinary coastal

landscapes like the great dune area of Foci del Rio Piscinas. Active dunes of gold-colored sand penetrate about three kilometers inland, blown by westerly winds, while junipers and tenacious pioneer vegetation futilely try to halt the advancing sand. Farther north, the long peninsula of Capo Frasca closes off the end of the Gulf of Oristano. Here on the military firing range F104's flash by, and it is said that at least one lies on the floor of the Gulf of Oristano, a coveted wreck yet to be discovered. Capo San Marco with its ruins of Tharros projects out from Sinis to close off the gulf. The peninsula of Sinis is an extraordinary environment: the inland area is a succession of low hills and large marshes, which particularly in spring offer unforgettable images. The eight thousand flamingos of Sal'e Porcus, a pink streak on the diaphanous waters of the marsh in the red light of sunset, are a spectacle that is alone worth the entire trip. The coast is a succession of calcareous cliffs and sandy beaches - but this is no common sand. Billions of small, measured

granules of quartzite embellish the beaches of Mari Ermi and Is Arutas. The reef of Catalano and the island of Mal di Ventre with its interesting, often wind-swept seabeds emerge off the mixed seabeds of rock, detritus and Neptune grass. Mal di Ventre is perhaps most well-known for its Roman ship sunk with a load of lead bars. Certainly the merchant who lost this precious cargo never imagined that two thousand years later his lead would make a great contribution to scientific research on the physics of matter. Indeed, two of those bars, which contain no radioactivity due to the long period they have remained underwater, were utilized in the laboratory of Gran Sasso in studies of atomic particles. Passing Capo Mannu, you begin another stretch of coast which is in large part intact and where several diving areas are becoming famous. One example is the reef of Su Puntillone, a steep pinnacle that carries another exotic touch of the Atlantic. Indeed, here you can observe sea tangles, a class of algae which is certainly not a common sight in the Mediterranean.

C

D

C - The islet of Ogliastra in the Gulf of Tortolì marks the transition from the limestone walls of the Gulf of Orosei to the granite of the southern coast.

D - A small white lighthouse overlooks the southern wall of Toro Island. The island marks the southernmost tip of Sardinia, and is only accessible when the weather is good.

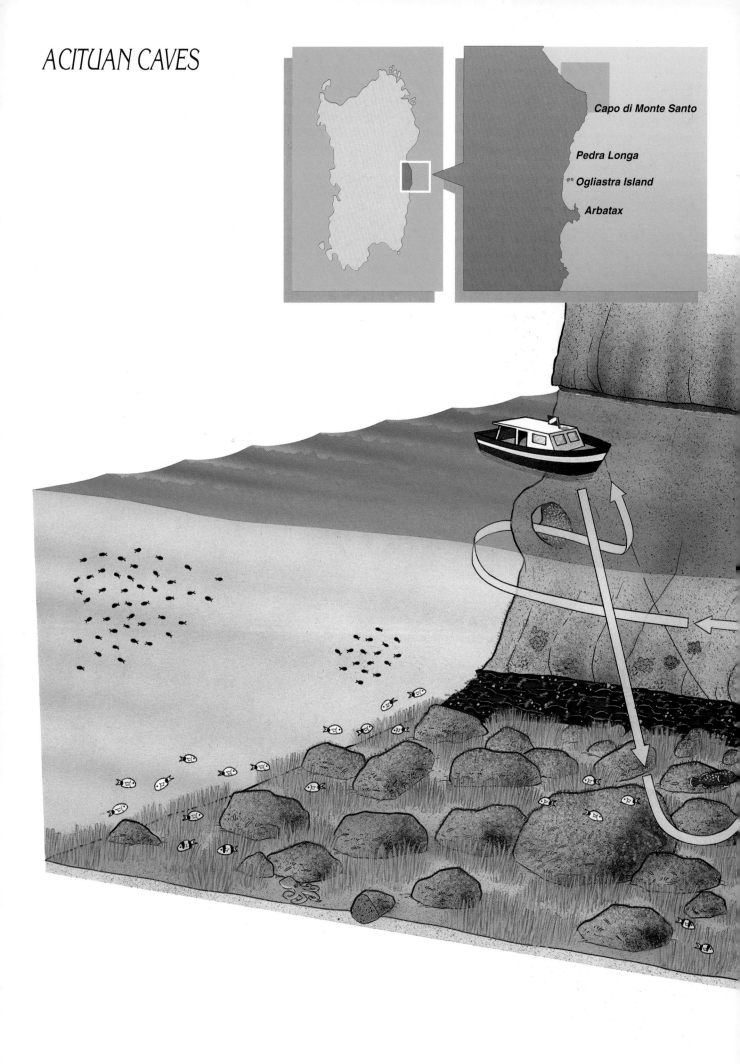

ACITUAN CAVES

Capo di Monte Santo

Pedra Longa

Ogliastra Island

Arbatax

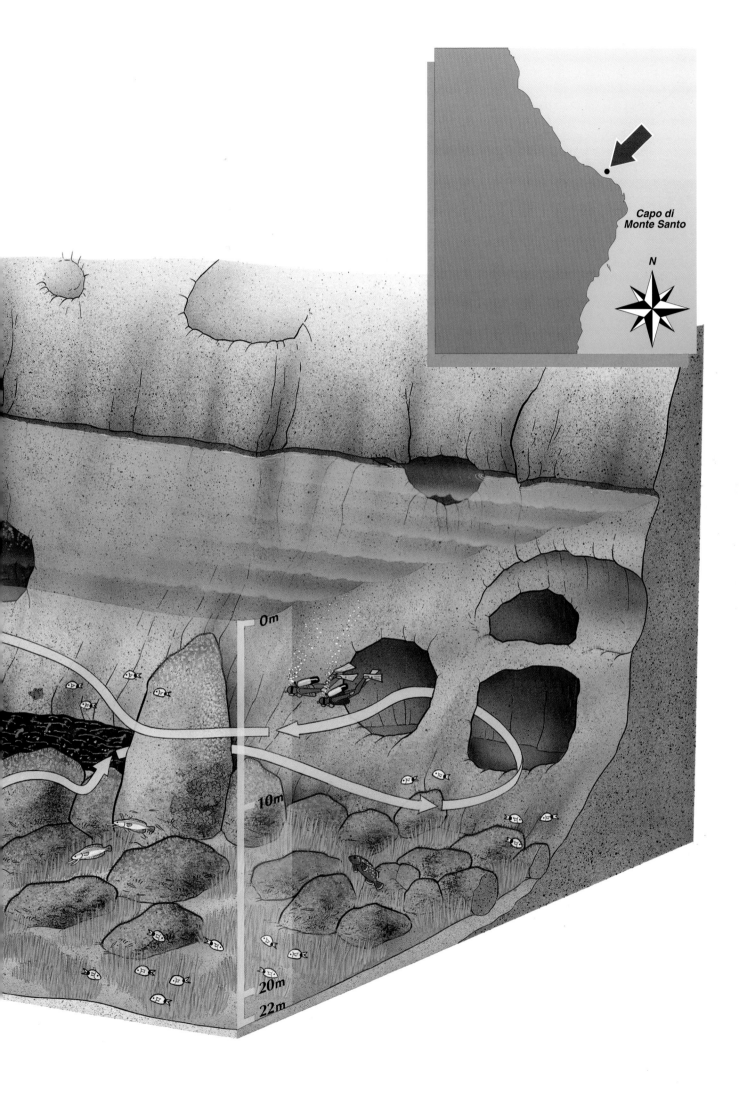

Capo di
Monte Santo

N

0m

10m

20m
22m

North of Capo di Monte Santu a series of inlets breaks the continuity of the low cliff: first Portu Pedrosu, then Portu Quau, and finally Porto Iltiera. Immediately afterwards, the wall rapidly rises until it exceeds 200 meters in height, dropping sheer into the sea.

Moor your boat here on a seabed of mixed rock and sand about 22 meters deep.

The wall faces northeast, and the best hours for diving are in the early morning, because later the sun disappears and the whole diving area falls into shadow. In addition, when the sun is still low on the horizon it shines directly into the caves, creating

A

of shadow and light.

The interior of the cave is covered with typical organisms such as corals, sponges, bryozoans and polychaete worms. In late spring and early summer many squills gather in the cave for reproduction, and then return to deeper waters.

Turning left toward the crevice, you will immediately see the other two openings: the smallest is almost on the surface, while the other, which is perfectly circular, leads back to the wall at a depth of about 8 meters.

From here return to the boat, keeping the wall to your right: despite the shallow depth, due to the only brief periods of light this

B

C

D

beautiful plays of shadow and light. The dive begins on the deeper rock masses, where rather large white seabreams often can be seen. In the crevices forkbeards and small groupers can be seen, and in early summer you may encounter large octopuses.

In an environment characterized by red algae, ascend to a depth of 18 meters and come to a large oblong mass resting on the wall, with its base surrounded by smaller rocks.

The passage between the mass and the wall is carpeted by brightly colored sponges, retepora and other bryozoans.

Coming out of the small tunnel, skirt the wall where the many

species of sponges include acanthellae with their jagged forms. Sometimes in summer you may find a specialized predator on one of the sponges: known as *Phyllidia flava*, this golden nudibranch, uncommon in the Mediterranean, is a beautiful yellow color with raised white spots. A few meters farther on are the entrances to the caves, or rather the cave, because the four openings are connected.

The main entrance to the cavity is about 10 meters deep and is divided in two by a rock bridge. From the interior looking out the scene is quite lovely: the rays of the sun pass through the upper opening, creating beautiful plays

A - *Due to the position of the wall, this area receives only a few hours of light daily, and the sun illuminates the entry of the caves only during the early morning. The wall is covered with sciophilous organisms and algae typical of areas with strong hydrodynamics.*

B - *The Gulf of Orosei is closed off to the south by Capo di Monte Santu. At the end of the gulf the walls become higher and plunge down into the depths, traversed by innumerable cavities.*

C - *The cavity has three connected entrances that form lovely plays of light and shadow when the sun is still low on the horizon.*

D - *The walls of the cave in the outer areas are covered with sponges, corals, bryozoans and annelids. Algae are completely absent due to lack of light.*

E - *The shallowest entrance is almost at the surface. The carpet of organisms on the walls grows increasingly sparse as you proceed into the cavity.*

F - *At the base of the cliff the flashlight beam illuminates red algae, numerous yellow sponges and green sea cactuses and sea fans.*

G - *A grouper seeks refuge in a cavity in the wall: in ambient lighting, the colors of this yellow-spotted fish are actually quite mimetic.*

H - *Red stars (Echinaster sepositus) are the most common species on the Sardinian seabeds.*

is a classic precoralligenous environment. Here along the wall the seascape changes with the seasons. During the winter the brown algae degrade and the various species of red algae predominate.

In spring sunlight increases and the brown algae begin to grow again, especially *Dictyopteris*, which covers over the winter carpet. In late summer, on the upper areas of wall near the surface, the rock seems alive with the drifting fronds of brown algae that add movement to color.

Your slow ascent to the surface will be an extremely entertaining exploration: crevices, holes and fissures alternate on the wall, and

E

inside you can observe an endless array of organisms. Predominating at depths of 5 meters to the surface are golden zoanthids, which stand out on the red of the sea roses and other algae. Almost at surface level, a little rock arch is carpeted with golden zoanthids and bryozoans, and often a small grouper seems to play hide-and-seek.

Emerge at the wall with the boat a few meters away. In late summer don't forget to look up - you will see one of the most extraordinary natural sights in the Mediterranean. In fact, this area is one of the few nesting places of the eleonora falcon, a rare and extremely elegant species.

F

G

H

SECCA DELL'ISOLOTTO

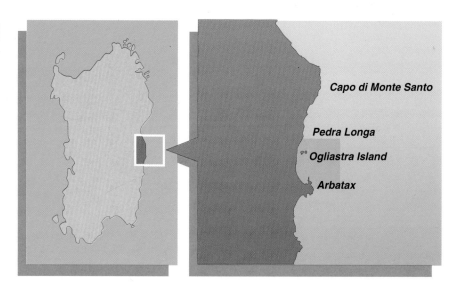

Capo di Monte Santo

Pedra Longa

Ogliastra Island

Arbatax

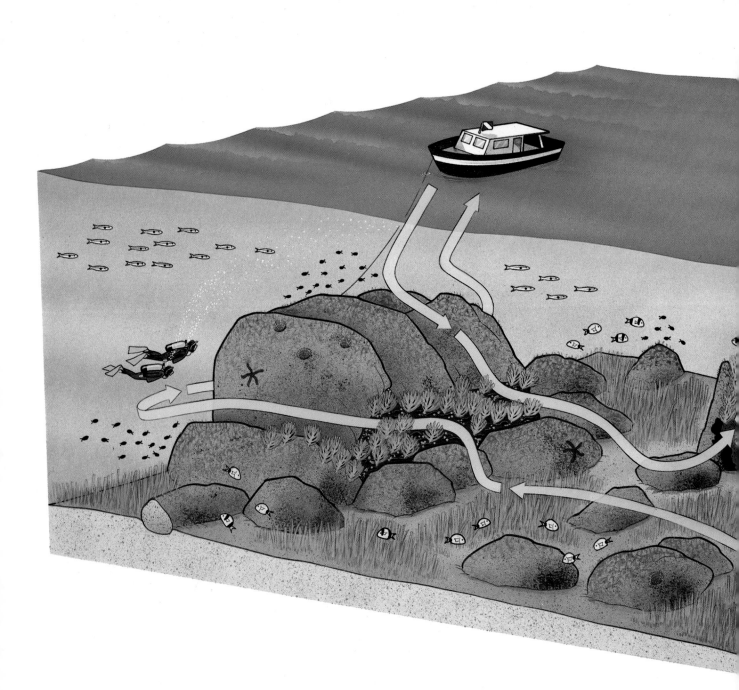

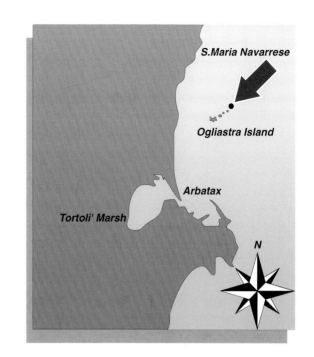

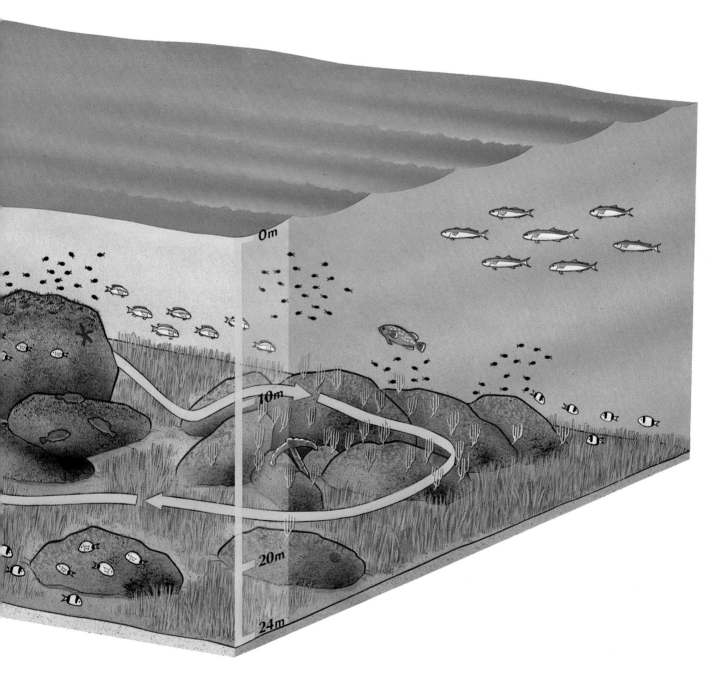

E - The Neptune grass that grows on the sea floor near the bow area of the wreck has also colonized the wreckage.

F - The outer side of the bottom of the ship is covered by colorful invertebrates, and many species of fish have found shelter below the wreckage.

Very little can be made out: a few pipes turned upward are somewhat of a sight.

The highest is 9 meters deep, and all are covered with luxuriant colonies of hydrozoans where colorful nudibranchs often graze. *Cratena*, *Flabellina* and *Coryphelia*, which feed on the polyps of hydrozoans, are the most common genera.

Colonies of *cnidaria* are common in many other areas of the wreck, which due to its somewhat elevated position on the flat sea

H

E

I

F

G

floor is often swept by currents. In general, the wreck has become a refuge for a large variety of organisms, some of which are rather rare, such as the long-spined urchin (*Centrostephanus longispinus*) hidden under the right side of the ship bottom. You may also see a few echinoderms (*Antedon mediterranea*), and if you look carefully among its tentacles you may spot a tiny symbiotic shrimp, perfectly camouflaged. Octopuses and small groupers hide among the wreckage, wrasses make their nests there and numerous orange and blue sponges find surfaces to grow on.

This very quantity and variety of organisms scattered on the wreckage and the small but luxuriant meadow that covers a portion of the wreck are what makes this dive interesting, a sort of revenge for the tragedy that caused its sinking and the rending explosions that almost totally destroyed it.

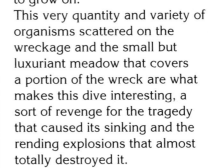

G - Despite the shallow depth, a flashlight is indispensable in order to observe the organisms that live under the wreckage.

H - The hull of the Entella *offers innumerable shelters for various organisms. Many octopuses make their lairs among the wreckage, where they hunt at night.*

I - Sea lilies (Antedon mediterranea) can be seen among the wreckage of the ship and on the Neptune grass. These organisms usually live attached to a support through the cirri located on their undersides, but they can also swim, elegantly moving their long arms.

79

THE WRECK OF THE ROMAGNA

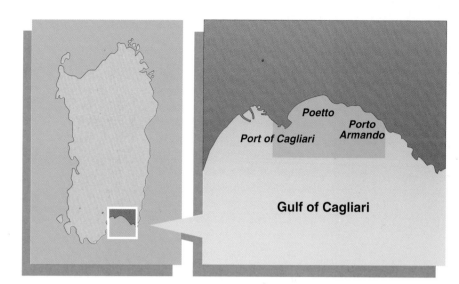

0m

10m

20m

30m

40 m

43 m

Molentargius

Quartu Salt Marshes

Poetto Beach

Porto Armando

Capo S.Elia

N

A

The *Romagna* was an old 1416 ton tanker built in 1899 which was requisitioned by the Navy to Cagliari on October 4, 1941. On August 2, 1943 the oil tanker was transporting its precious cargo of fuel to Cagliari, where it was of strategic military importance, especially for the air force, which was engaged in defending the island.

The *Romagna* was escorted by six small antisubmarines and two pairs of Macchi 202 and 205.

At eight o'clock in the morning, when it was only a few miles from the port of Cagliari, the *Romagna* plowed into a mine from a mine defense that had been recently placed and of which land positions had probably not advised the tanker: since the beginning of the war, over 5,000 mines had been placed in minefields in the Gulf of Cagliari and along the Sardinian coast. The explosion of the device blew away the bow and caused the fuel to ignite. The ship, stopped in its tracks, then foundered out of control. The *Romagna*, completely devastated by the fire and the explosion of the fuel, sank about a kilometer away from the point where it ran into the mine.

Today it lies upright in the sand, about a hundred meters long, looking almost as if it were ready to sail again as it was when it was stopped by the mine that tore the bow from the rest of the ship.

Go down twenty meters along the mooring line in totally blue waters until the enormous form of the *Romagna* suddenly appears 15 meters farther below.

The highest sections are 32 meters deep. Almost everything has collapsed on the deck, including the great yards and the smokestacks, while only the lower parts of the cabins remain. Near the stern the wreckage seems held together by a myriad of nets and ropes: be very careful not to get entangled in them.

Leaning out of the hull, the sense of enormity increases.

Descend to the aft bottom, more than ten meters below, and the sight of the enormous propeller and the rudder alone makes the dive worthwhile. The blades are longer than a man and the rudder is 5 or 6 meters high. The view from below is truly spectacular. The wreck is enveloped in a cloud of anthias, while the sandy sea floor is a carpet of black bristlestars. Coming back to the deck, it is not easy to decipher the contorted wreckage and what it once was.

A good number of dives are necessary to get an overall view. Tall sargassum grass, some of it 50 centimeters high, grows on the wreckage, while every so often a school of large white seabreams passes by, and several good size scorpionfish lie in wait, motionless. Large conger eels and morays hide in the pipes and scrap.

B

C

D

A - The *Romagna* is lying on a sandy seabed that in many areas is covered by a myriad of black bristlestars. These starfish, which at times are crowded around the same prey, provide a most unusual sight.

B - The view of the imposing stern of the *Romagna* may be the most impressive moment of the entire dive. A comparison with the size of the diver reveals its enormity.

C - The rudder and the blade of the propeller are still in place. A photograph with a diver shows how enormous the blades of the ship actually are. The projecting curve of the transom can also be seen.

D - The *Romagna* is popular not only with divers, but also with fishing enthusiasts. Unfortunately, the result is a tangle of nets and ropes that envelopes the structure of the stern.

E - The Romagna was an oil tanker and had few structures on the deck. Most of them have been destroyed, except for this small cabin.

F - The bow of the Romagna is about 800 meters away from the hull. A large anchor, its fluke covered by sponges, pokes out of the right hawsehole.

G - The entire wreck is surrounded by clouds of swallowtail sea perches (Anthias anthias) small fish typical of deep shallows.

H - The bow area is the most devastated. This is where the ship hit the mine, and where the explosion tore the tip of the ship completely off. The bow was further damaged by fires.

I - It is possible to visit some internal parts of the bow, a number of holds and the small cabin on the deck. Special safety measures are of course necessary to enter the ship, which should be explored only by very expert divers.

F

completely torn off.

On the sand before the bow sparse accumulations of materials are partially submerged and difficult to decipher. Here as well, an extraordinary concentration of black bristlestars cover the bottom: some are grouped on top of their prey. The stump of the bow is too far from the hull to reach during this dive, but if it were possible there would be no problems in orientation because a long strip of wreckage and fragments seems to connect the two pieces of the ship.

Another dive is necessary to see this part of the ship, and it is like diving on another wreck. It lies 43 meters deep and is enveloped by a cloud of red damselfish.

Here as well, the left side is torn apart, and the contorted wreckage shows the point of impact with the mine.

The right side looks like it was cut with a blowtorch, and from the hawsehole a long chain hangs to which the anchor is still attached, resting on the sandy seabed.

A couple of meters away a large moray pokes its head out from the wreckage. The small portion of deck remaining is covered with wood, like the hull of the *Romagna*. Inside the wreckage a good-sized school of large seabreams takes refuge.

Like all large sunken wrecks, the *Romagna* offers new discoveries and thrills with every dive.

E

G

On a bulkhead of the deck is a spare anchor, while farther on is a bathtub: what it is doing here is a mystery. Perhaps it was in a bathroom uncovered by the explosions. The ceiling and walls are in fact missing.

The left broadside seems swollen: probably the explosions and the enormous heat of the fire deformed the thick plates.

The long yards are lying on the deck, and that of the bow is drooping in the large gash caused by the mine. At the point of impact, on the left side of the bow, enormous contorted wreckage scattered throughout is a clear indication of the violence of the explosion. The right side seems

H

I

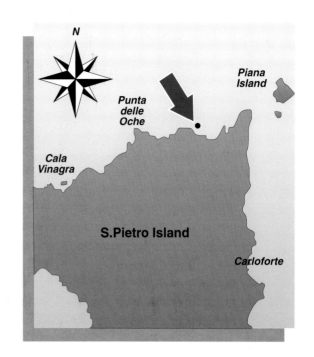

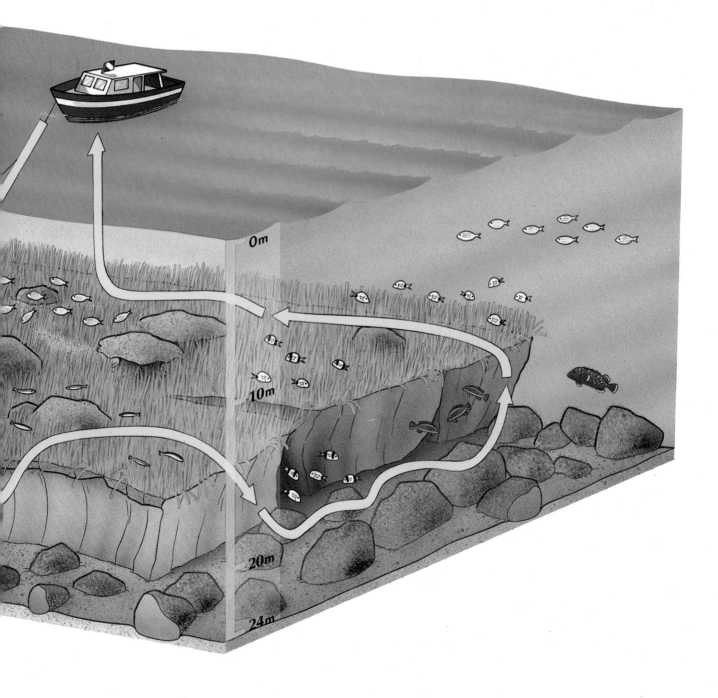

ailing along the coast of Carloforte from the east, after passing the tuna fisheries, still in partial use, you will note distant layers of light sedimentary rock standing out on the dark volcanic walls toward the northwest. This is Tacche Bianche, and it is the area where the tuna fishing nets were once located.

The present day tuna nets, which are once again in use, are set down in the spring only a few hundred meters farther east. Moor the boat about 200 meters from the shore, on a seabed which does not appear extremely attractive. At a depth of 18 meters a flat area covered by a dense meadow of Neptune grass is

A

interrupted here and there by scattered rounded masses and strange, mushroom-shaped rocky formations. Toward the open sea the plateau is broken by a rockslide of large square blocks of light rock which form an endless number of crevices. Descend along the mooring line and suddenly a large rounded opening with smooth walls appears in the meadow. Go in, and you will unexpectedly find yourself at the entrance to a large, wide tunnel that runs under the meadow. In various areas the vault has collapsed, and the masses that stand in the passage without blocking the wall permit light to enter. The floor of the tunnel

B

D

C

reaches a maximum depth of 24 meters and is covered by smooth rocks with pink patches of encrusting red algae that alternate with areas of light sand.

The walls and the vaults in the less illuminated areas are almost bare, while near the openings broad colorful patches of sponges appear. The tunnel is a favorite habitat of squills, which in late spring are quite common here. The tunnel continues for dozens of meters, with columns and other rockslides, until a pile of rocks closes the passageway and you come out onto the meadow above. As you come out, be careful of your movements, as it is easy to surprise not only the ever-present

A - Channels created by karst phenomena run under the surface covered by Neptune grass, while on the sea floor there are rocky masses and white sand. Large openings connect the two levels and create fascinating plays of light.

B - A number of light-colored sedimentary deposits stand out among the dark volcanic rocks on the north side of S. Pietro Island, known as Tacche Bianche.

C - The meadow of Neptune grass that covers the sea floor is broken by rockslides, and the colors explode at the base of the rocky masses. A red star crawls on a carpet of brightly-colored invertebrates.

D - The meadow of Neptune gras is inhabited by a myriad of fish and invertebrates.

E - These sea fans are small green algae typical of areas with poor illumination.

F - Every part of the meadow of Neptune grass is inhabited by organisms: a hermit crab crawls along its leaves, which have been colonized by red algae and bryozoans.

G - The sharpsnout seabream (Diplodus puntazzo) is easily distinguished from other seabreams by its clear vertical streaks and prominent mouth.

H - The blotched pickerel (Spicara maena) prefers Neptune grass meadows for its reproduction ground.

I - Cuttlefish are quite common in all shallow areas.

schools of salemas, but also a big gilt-head bream or a large common seabream.
The plateau hides other tunnels which are easily accessible, but be careful to check your computer often. The depth of the dive is constant and considering the maximum depth, downtime is rather brief and passes quite quickly as you wander through the tunnels. At the end of the plateau there is a sheer edge with smooth walls that connect numerous tunnels of various size. Here at the foot of the wall, among the rockslides and the crevices, beautiful groupers and large brown meagres can easily be seen. Seabreams also find shelter in the

deeper areas. While the lower level is quite interesting, so is the meadow above it, scattered with strange-shaped, eroded and fissured masses.
One of these looks like an airplane with wings and cockpit.
Green and rainbow wrasses, black seabreams and two-banded seabreams swim among the tufts of Neptune grass, and if you look for smaller species you will see crustaceans, tube dwelling anemones, sea anemones, spirographs, ascidians and bryozoans. Once again, an apparently monotonous, uninteresting environment reveals a rich variety in forms of life and unexpected seascapes.

F
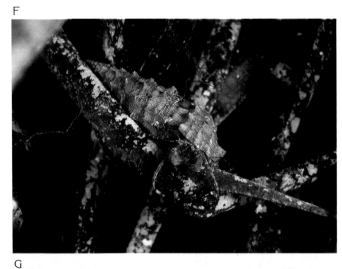

G

H

I

99

S'ARCHITTU

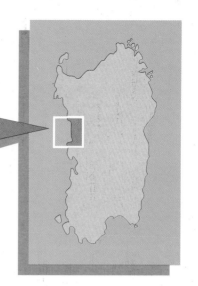

Capo Marargiu

Bosa

Torre Columbargia
Corona Niedda Rock
Punta Foghe
Capo Nieddu

S.Caterina di Pittinuri
S'Archittu

Capo Mannu

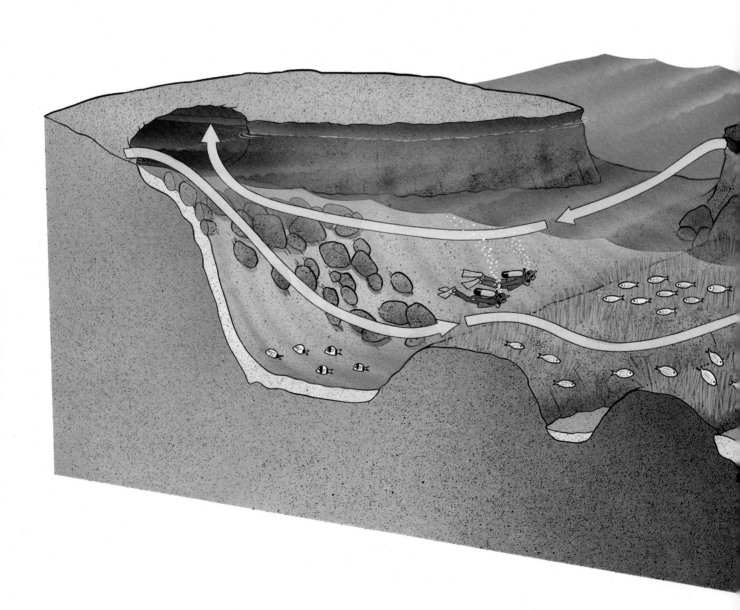

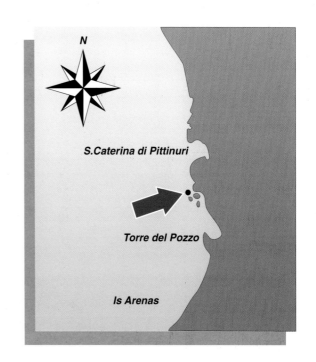

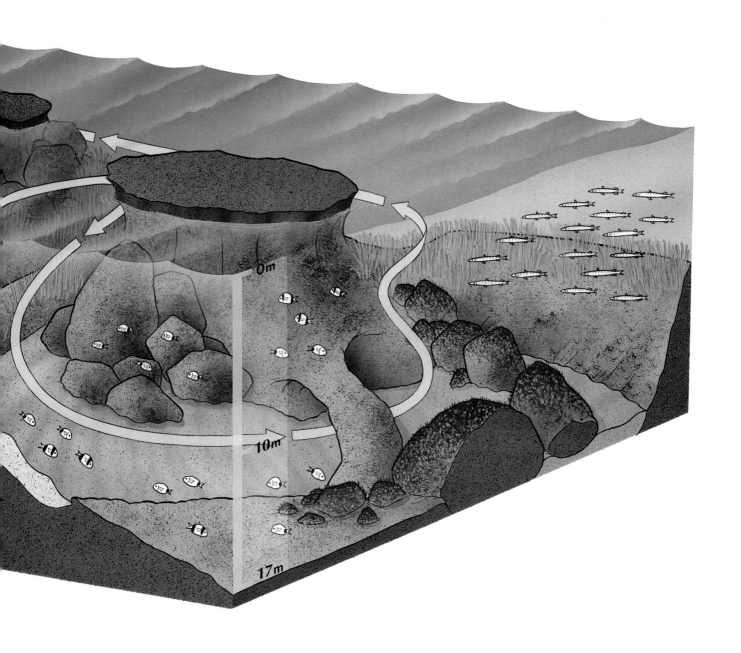

0m

10m

17m

A

B

C

A - The promontory of S'Archittu juts out to the north of the Sinis Peninsula. The sandstone that forms it has been eroded by the waves and the sea. The dive begins right under the natural arch.

B - The erosion phenomena that have transformed the rocks in the area are evident under water as well. Vaults, tunnels and channels can be seen that make the dive quite varied and beautiful.

C - Neptune grass colonizes many channels among the rocks, and sometimes grows luxuriantly even above the blocks of sandstone. The abrupt transition from the Neptune grass to the red algae is quite striking.

D - A horse pipefish (Sygnatus typhle) shows off its extraordinary mimetic skills, not only standing erect, like the leaves of the Neptune grass, but also faithfully reproducing its color.

E - A sea lily distends its arms among a pile of dead Neptune grass leaves, in another quite remarkable feat of mimicry.

Walls of sandstone begin as you head north up the coast past Sinis, passing the large sandy inlet of Is Arenas. The rock has been sculpted by the wind and water, and the symbol of the coastal landscape of this area is S'Archittu, a large natural vault traversed from end to end by the sea. The dive begins right here, from the land side of the tunnel. Descend a few meters deep, passing rapidly from a well-illuminated environment to the tunnel, where red algae thickly coats the walls and the floor. Sand and smooth rock masses show signs of strong hydrodynamics, and the sediment is distributed in parallel waves.

The red algae are primarily coralline, with various encrusting species. The long tunnel is lovely, especially due to the light that enters from the two entrances. It leads out onto a sandy flat area surrounded by thick patches of Neptune grass. The long diving route begins here, through channels, vaults and passage holes, leading around the two emerging reefs just off from the cape. The seabed, like the rest of the surrounding area, is marked by the erosion processes which affected the coast when it lay above water. Remains of karst conduits form beautiful passages carved in the crumbling rocks, where erosion continues with the constant currents. The higher zones are covered with Neptune grass, which has also colonized many sandy channels. Heart urchins, especially those from the genus *Echinocardium*, live buried in the sediment, with their thin exoskeleton covered with thick hairs. Go past the first rise, where thick schools of salemas graze on the Neptune grass. Then head left to a channel 12 meters deep, and come to the side of the largest emerging reef facing the shore. To the side of the reef a hole leads into a vertical well with a floor about 14 meters deep, covered by large smooth stones. Exit from a vault covered with golden zoanthids. Move with caution, as it is not uncommon to encounter amberjacks, leer-fish or even bass.

D

Right as you exit go around a pile of masses at the base of the reef, to enter into another channel with a sandy floor. The walls are covered with corals, and on the edges grow numerous colonies of hydrozoans. Just a little farther up is the Neptune grass meadow that borders the sciophilous areas. The channel is interrupted by an arch: after crossing it you will see scattered masses, where white seabreams and two-banded seabreams are swimming. Turn left again and, after crossing

F - A colorful sea slug (Tylodina perversa) *feeds on its favorite sponge* (Aplysina aerophoba). *The slug is unmistakable due to its showy yellow color and its pagoda-shaped shell.*

E

H

F

another nearby arch, on the wall of the reef you will see a rise covered with Neptune grass. Go past it and, going around the rock, head back, aiming for the other small emerging reef.

Come out toward the shore and go to the wall that once again leads under the tunnel you started from, go back along it and come out on the shallows.

The most entertaining aspect of this dive is the continuing variety of the seascape and the many passages among the rocks.

Moreover, it is an extremely easy dive, although you should always be careful of your position in the channels and tunnels.

There is much to see. For those interested in nudibranchs, some uncommon species such as *Berghia caerulescens* and *Calmella cavolinii*, two small, colorful members of the Eolidacea family, are common here. On the walls of the channels you may also see some beautiful lobsters.

But the crowning touch, if you are lucky, could be a fine school of barracudas.

G - The pearly razor fish (Xyrichthys novacula) *lives in patches of sand. Its fine colors appear evanescent against the sand. The pearly razor fish often hides in the sand to escape from predators.*

H - Sea anemones (Anemonia sulcata) *are common in the meadows and among the rocks. Sea anemones can become quite large: the crown of tentacles is always visible, while the column is hidden.*

G

SU PUNTILLONE

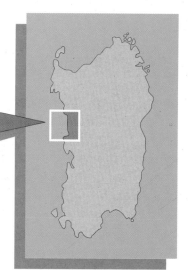

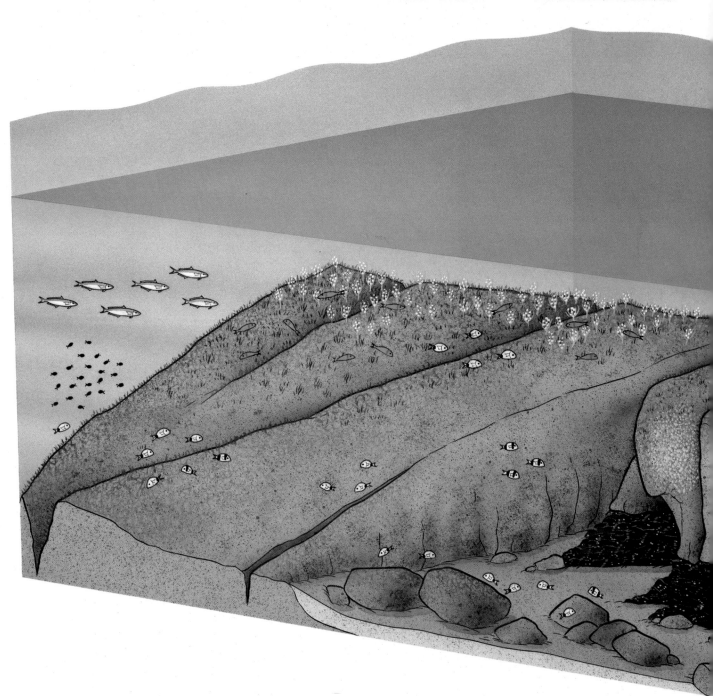

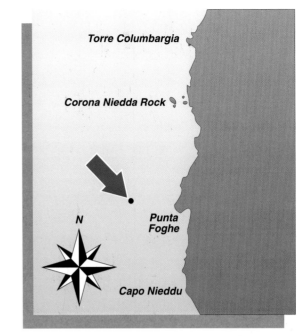

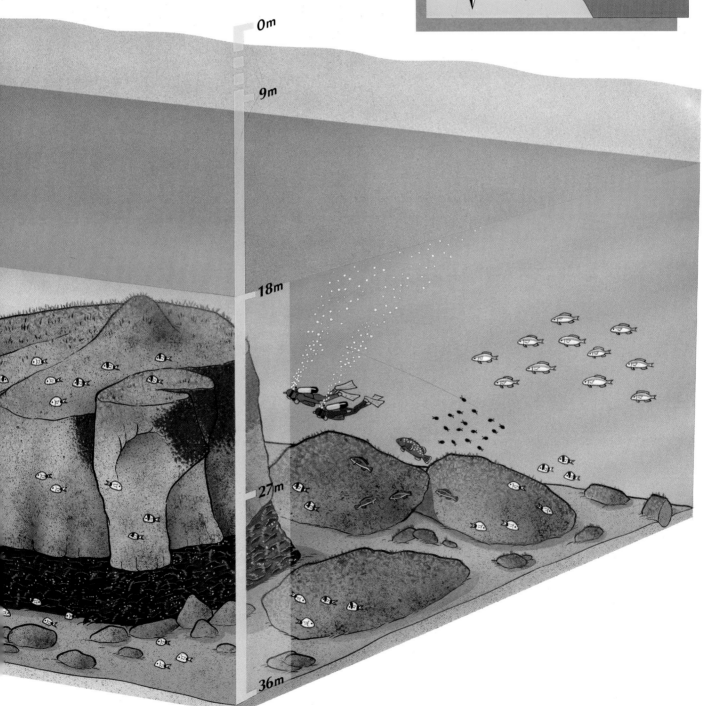

cave were completely covered with red coral, but uncontrolled fishing has left only a few colonies in a few points of the cavern, and among the sediments on the floor only a few fragments remain of what must have been a true treasure, hundreds of kilos of fossil coral fallen from the vault. Descending along the cliff to the largest opening and entering the cavern, you will see a continuous sequence of changes in the composition of the organisms that cover the rock as illumination gradually decreases. On the outside on the masses on the sea floor, covered with a low mantle of photophilic algae, salemas graze and saddled seabreams and other breams swim about. On the walls where the tunnels open out there is a typical cliff environment with moderately sciophilous algae such as sea cactus and sea fans. The succession continues, with golden zoanthids which are then replaced by *Leptosammia pruvoti*: among these, in addition to the sparse branches of coral, are jumbles of sponges, bryozoans, annelids and sea anemones, while the algae

disappears completely in the absence of light. At the entrance of the conduits there are large rock violets (*Microcosmus sp.*) with an almost unrecognizable rough body, covered as they are with other animals, especially sponges. Specialized predators like the little *Hypselodoris tricolor* graze on the sponges, while the nudibranch gastropod *Discodoris atromaculata* grazes on *Petrosia*, which in the cave environment appears whitish due to the absence of the symbiotic algae present when there is light. This is also the typical environment for many crustaceans such as the porter crab with its robust pink claws, which grow quite large here, spiny lobsters, *Herbstia condyliata* crabs, and squat lobsters. In the inner areas live large lobsters and narval shrimp, elegant with their long beaks and fine white antennae and sometimes gathering in large crowds. In the cave there are also cleaning stations for the banded shrimp (*Stenopus spinosus*) with its long white antennae. Seen only in dark caves, this shrimp offers its services to complacent, quite large

H - Leptosammia pruvoti *is a coral typical of poorly illuminated areas and covers entire walls at the entrance to cavities* *and crevices. Each individual has a hard calcareous skeleton, with the same yellow color as its tentacles.*

G

H

brown meagres that occupy several deep recesses in the cave. Another exclusive inhabitant of caves is a small brown fish with a snub nose: it is known as *Oligopus ater*, and as may be guessed, its name describes it well. *Oligopus* comes from the fact that instead of having distinct dorsal, caudal and anal fins like other fish, it has a single large fin that goes from back to stomach. *Ater* comes from its nearly black color. In addition to these animals capable of movement, all the sedentary organisms which live on the walls are either suspension feeders or filtrators: that is, they use different systems to collect the particles carried in by the current, and release waste that falls onto the seabed. This explains the presence of large tube-dwelling anemones, encouraged by the continuous fall of fine material. The cave holds surprises by night as well. Often large dentex come in from the open sea to sleep in the cavities, and this is the only time when these mysterious pelagic predators will permit divers to approach.

*E - A small red scorpionfish (*Scorpaena notata*) camouflages itself against the rock. Like larger scorpionfish, it uses mimicry both as a defense and to make itself invisible to prey.*

*F - A porter crab (*Dromia personata*) moves along the wall of a cavern in Nereo Cave. Its name comes from the fact that, especially when small, it carries a fragment of sponge on its carapace which it uses to hide itself.*

*G - Dark cavities are a typical habitat of cardinal fish (*Apogon imberbis*), swarms of which occupy them.*

E

F

SECCA DI PORTO LECCIO

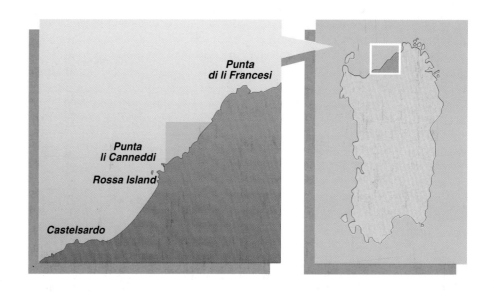

Punta di li Francesi

Punta li Canneddi

Rossa Island

Castelsardo

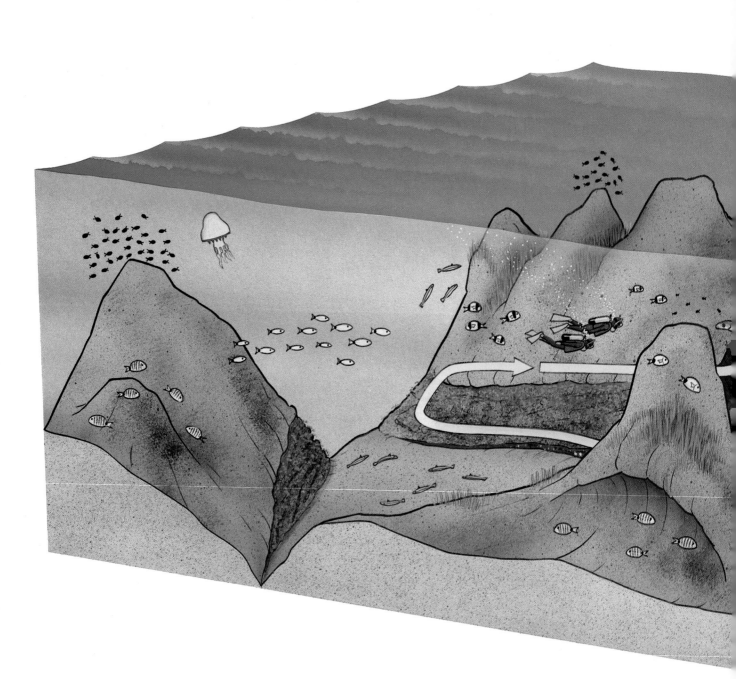

Cala Sarraina

Costa Paradiso

Porto Leccio

Punta
li Canneddi

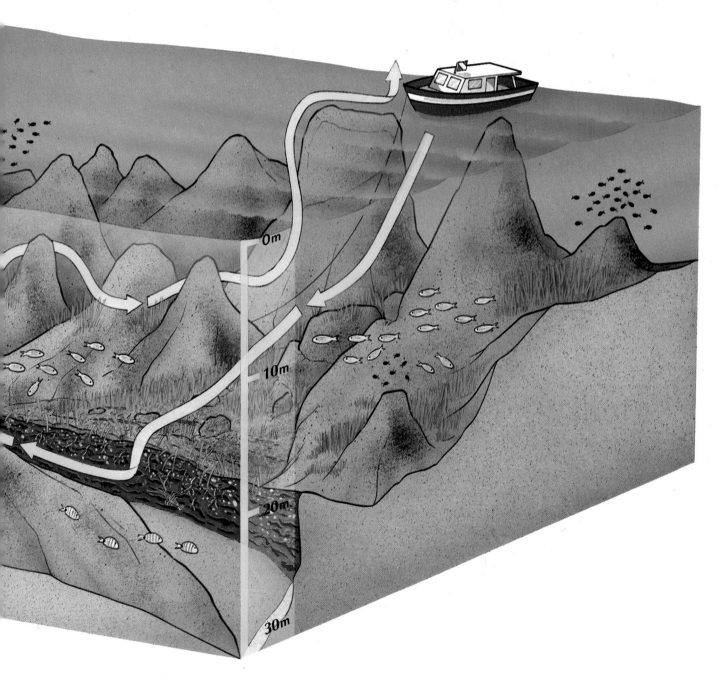

0m

10m

20m

30m

A

B

C

D

Costa Paradiso is a tourist resort located on the northern coast between Castelsardo and Vignola. The coast is rocky and jagged, with reddish granite interrupted by low vegetation that surrounds small sandy inlets. A rocky promontory, surrounded by rocks and emerging shallows, protrudes out to sea between the bay of Li Cossi and that of Porto Leccio. To the west of the point several submerged peaks rise to 3 meters from the surface: this is where you should throw your anchor. The two tallest spurs are close to each other and divided by a trough that makes them look like two horns. This is why the place is also known as Secca del Vichingo.

E

Between the two peaks you will first encounter rocky masses, then, turning to the right, the sea floor widens and, at a depth from ten to twenty meters, there is a strange mixture of patches of Neptune grass and a coralligenous seabed with deep cracks, fissures and holes. The superficial layer is formed by sea cactus, and right below it is an imposing mass constructed by red algae. The short descent leads to a deeper area on the sand, to a depth of 31 meters. To the left, however, from twenty meters down and deeper, the wall descends vertically and leads into a narrow channel with a sandy bottom. The other side of the channel is formed by the base of

A - Most of the dive at Secca di Porto Leccio is along a deep channel with walls covered by large coralligenous formations.

B - The upper portion of the shallow is colonized by sparse patches of Neptune grass.

C - The uppermost rocks of the shallow are frequented by large schools of salemas, which graze among the algae.

D - The less exposed areas of the channel are covered by a layer of red algae, especially sea roses. Throughout the dive, the transition from illuminated to shaded areas is marked by abrupt changes in environment.

E - The decrease in light from the upper portion of the shallow to the central channel is evident, making a flashlight necessary.

F - Beautiful colonies of red coral grow among the red algae on the walls.

G - The coralligenous environment includes an intricate combination of organisms heaped on top of each other. The green thalli of the sea cactus grow above them all.

H - A female black-faced blenny (Trypterigion tripteronotus) hovers motionless among the algae in wait of small prey.

I - The lobster's preferred habitat is within the coralligenous crevices.

another rocky emergence which is overlooked by a pointed spur that rises to a depth of 7 meters. The walls of the channel are carpeted with concretions of red algae. In fact, the light fades almost abruptly, creating a very particular situation. The edge of the channel is in part colonized by Neptune grass, and right under the roots of the phanerogams grows red coral. The small colonies of coral are quite numerous in the crevices and under the vaults, along with a large variety of other organisms typical of dark areas: sponges, bryozoans and annelids carpet every bit of available space, even climbing on top of each other. This is also a common habitat for spiny lobsters:

F

G

I

dozens of antennae poke out of the holes, and some of them belong to quite large specimens. Among the sponges you can see various species of nudibranchs, squat lobsters barely poke out from the fissures, while in the deeper holes, especially in early summer, you can see squills. Keep an eye on your gauge and computer as you cross the channel, because you are exploring at a depth of 27 meters, and there are so many things to see that it is easy to lose track of time. Ascend along a cleft covered with corals, crossed by a fissure where you can see seabreams and conger eels. As you reach shallower depths, at the base of the peaks between 10 and 15 meters deep, large schools of

salemas, seabreams and beautiful saddled seabreams swim among patches of Neptune grass and coral and emerged rocks. On the various species of algae you are likely to encounter small grazing species: sea slugs from the Sacoglossa order, like the brightly colored *Thuridilla hopei* and the mimetic *Elysia viridis*. The latter favors the branching fronds of codium algae, a dark green algae covered with thick fuzz. Before leaving the water, your safety stop is a stroll from the top of one peak to another. This is a good way to enjoy the quite lively scene, to spot groups of jellyfish rocking gently, and, if you have a sharp eye, to see tiny nudibranchs hidden in the niches in dimmer areas.

E - Large red scorpionfish are common on the rocks of the seabed. This close-up shows the complicated appendages that break up the image of the fish, and its intricate pattern of colors.

granite protuberance. You will come out onto a channel among masses dominated by a pointed spire that rises diagonally toward the surface. The more sheltered side is covered by a carpet of golden zoanthids and red sponges from which the fans of the gorgonians rise. Following the spire toward the seabed, you enter naturally into a passage between the triangular-shaped masses. The red gorgonians grow not only on the walls, but also on the seabed, a clear sign that powerful currents sweep through

beautiful grouper. Sometimes a group of eagle rays seem to fly up from the patches of sand among the masses or from the flat rocky areas. They move away slowly, disturbed by the noise of the bubbles. Going on, the rock becomes sheer, like an enormous belly of granite, and among the golden zoanthids a large quantity of yellow sponges (*Alysina cavernicola*) replaces the gorgonians on the wall.
The structure of the shallow is so imposing that you almost do not

G - The sea fans are often surrounded by carpets of golden zoanthids and colorful sponges. Only the camera flash or a flashlight will reveal this explosion of colors.

F

G

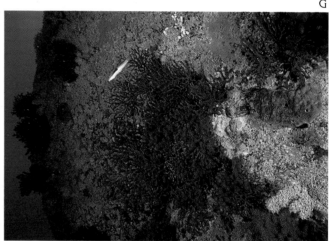

H

F - In certain areas along the vertical wall the sea fans are so thick that they form a small forest.
The gorgonians are all growing in the same direction.

this sort of natural tunnel. Come out onto a channel with a sandy floor surrounded by high rock walls. Following the channel to the left, you will come to the base of enormous blocks that form the central portion of the shallow. The scenery is imposing and the vertical walls in the shadows, seen by the beam of your flashlight, reveal the yellow of the golden zoanthids and the bright red of the gorgonians. In the fissures among the rocks hide large morays, and every so often you may see a

notice the extraordinary variety of organisms that cover the rock. Following the edge of the enormous hulk of rock, spiral up to the main plateau of the shallow, where little clouds of seabreams and schools of salemas move tranquilly about as they search for food among the algae that cover the masses.
The rocks below will still be visible during your brief safety stop before emerging, and as you climb back onto the boat and look at the surrounding islands, it seems a replica of the underwater scene.

H - When the polyps of the colonies of sea fans retract their tentacles, the gorgonian's appearance changes and it seems "thinner." Gorgonians with their polyps expanded are commonly considered to be "in flower," and it is no coincidence that the scientific name for these organisms means animals that look like flowers.

133

SECCA DEI MONACI

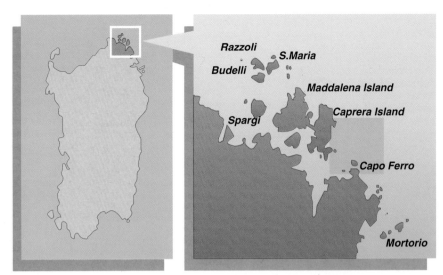

Razzoli
S.Maria
Budelli
Maddalena Island
Spargi
Caprera Island
Capo Ferro
Mortorio

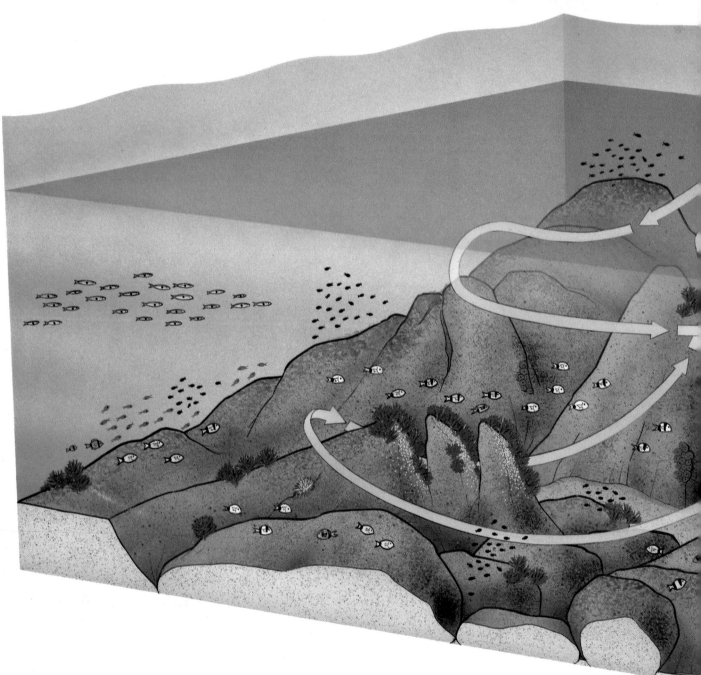

I Monaci

Secca dei Monaci

Caprera Island

Le Bisce

Capo Ferro

N

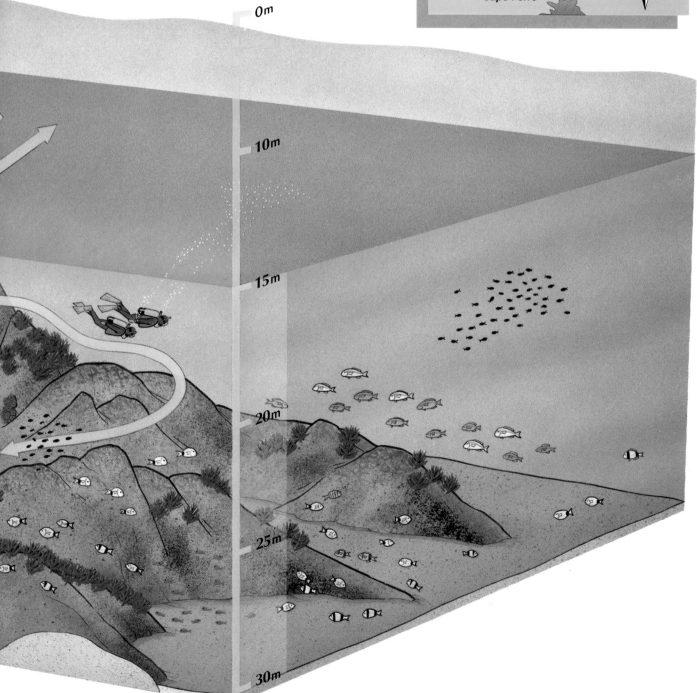

0m

10m

15m

20m

25m

30m

To the east of the island of Caprera a group of granite shoals forms the Secca dei Monaci, the only emerging area in a quite extensive group of shallows. On the largest shoal there is a small lantern, while on the one farther east a beacon marks other shoals that rise almost to the surface. To the north of the signal is the Secca di fuori, which has two shallower points at depths of 13 and 16 meters. When the sea is calm and the water is clear, you can easily see the tops of the reef from the surface. Anchor on the rocks at a depth of 16 meters. The shallow is formed of a group of granite blocks, often quite jagged. The usual cloud of damselfish surrounds the reef,

form spires and narrow clefts. Here there is a true explosion of color: the yellows of the golden zoanthids compete with the red gorgonians which cover entire walls and grow on both sides of the vertical cracks, nearly blocking the way. They are present in great numbers, and their fans are quite large. Dense schools of anthias swim among the sea fans. Although from a distance they appear to be a uniform pinkish red color, from close up males exhibit a complex coloration, with yellow, lilac and pink streaks. Male anthias can also be distinguished by their pectoral and dorsal fins, which are longer than those of the females, and by their generally greater size. As you observe the

A

B

and as you descend look around you into the blue depths and you are likely to see schools of dentex and amberjacks. Descend along the slope toward a sandy channel which, at a depth of 27 meters, separates the main rocks from another group of rocky shoals. From the very start the rock is covered with the usual low photophilic algae, but quite soon gorgonians make their appearance, at first sparse and then increasingly thick. In the less exposed areas carpets of golden zoanthids are interrupted by broad areas covered with sponges. They are all *Chondrosia reniformis*, and are more common in dark crevices than in such exposed areas. Passing the sandy channel, the deepest rocks

C

D

A - East of Caprera a small lighthouse marks the islet of Monaci, surrounded by a vast area of shallows. A beacon signals a group of almost emerging reefs, and a little to the north is the diving area.

B - The red gorgonians are the main attraction of the shallow. They grow densely here, with large fans on the deeper rocks, especially where the shape of the rocks channels the currents.

C - The concentration of gorgonians is a good indicator of hydrodynamics: probably growth is sparser where there are fewer feeding opportunities.

D - Despite the extraordinarily clear water and the bright light that penetrates to the depths, only the camera flash will bring out the brilliant red of the gorgonians, which otherwise appear to be a uniform dark blue.

gorgonians from below, take a look at the sea above as well, and you will immediately become aware that the water is so clear that you can see the boat moored almost 30 meters above. Many animals live on the gorgonians and take advantage of the favorable position: annelids from the genus *Filograna*, with their complicated masses of little white tubes, are common guests on the sea fans. Going around the spires, you will see a large sea anemone that hosts a whole community of inachus crabs: covered with algae, the inachus live like this, protected by the stinging cells of the sea anemone. Passing the spires, you will come to another rise: here as well, gorgonians and golden

E - A spur of rock is completely covered by golden zoanthids. The bright yellow of these small cnidarians sets off the red sea fans.

F - Gorgonians growing in cracks on both sides of the walls have blocked the way. Twenty-seven meters above, the light that penetrates from the surface rapidly changes from azure to dark blue.

G - The deepest are as of the shallow are inhabited by dense swarms of damselfish. Although they seem uniform in color, red damselfish actually are covered with delicate patterns and shades of color.

H - The upper portions of the shallow seem somewhat bare compared with the luxuriant forests of sea fans on the sea floor. But don't be fooled: large orange sponges and many other organisms create extremely interesting environments.

zoanthids cover the areas more exposed to the current. Ascend and come back toward the highest rocks. You will see groups of white and sharpsnout seabreams in search of food: on the top of the masses there are erect colonies of hydrozoans, grazed by various species of nudibranchs, especially *Coryphella*. After reaching the summit of the shallow, before you reemerge there is still time to look around into the blue depths. Often your bubbles will attract amberjacks, while dentex tend to keep their distance. Come up along the mooring line, and as you make your safety stop you will have an excellent overall view of this shallow, heightened by the exceptionally clear water.

Red sea fan - *Paramuricea clavata*

This is the classic red gorgonian. It forms branching fans up to one metre high, generally on a single level. Like coral, it is a colonial animal, but has a flexible horny skeleton. Its polyps are red. A bi-coloured variety exists in which the branches range from red to yellow and are rarely completely yellow. The bi-coloured colonies are quite localized.

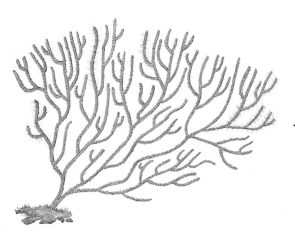

Yellow sea fan - *Eunicella cavolinii*

This is the yellow gorgonian, quite common at even shallow depths. It lives in areas with poor illumination and a fair level of hydrodynamics. It is generally quite branching and has a very flexible skeleton. It often hosts a small gastropod mollusk, *Neosimnia spelta*, which feeds on the polyps of the gorgonian. The mantle that covers the mollusk's shell is quite mimetic, making it difficult to distinguish from the tissues of the gorgonians.

White sea fan - *Eunicella singularis*

This is a white gorgonian with elongated threadlike branches, generally turned upwards. Under special circumstances it will form true carpets on both rocky and detrital seabeds. When it lives in well-illuminated areas, it has microscopic symbiotic algae in its tissues that give it a greenish colour. The polyps are always slightly darker.

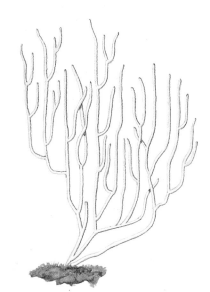

Dead man's finger - *Alcyonium palmatum*

This is a colonial animal that belongs to the same group as corals and gorgonians, but unlike these does not have a hard skeleton, and is instead supported by scattered spicules within the body of the colony. It is red or pinkish in colour and has small white polyps with eight pinnate tentacles. The colony develops on a primary stele with stumpy branches.

Encrusting alcionarian - *Parerythopodium coralloides*

This is a colonial alcyonacea similar to the soft corals of tropical seas. The colony's connective tissue is red, while the polyps are yellow with white tentacles. Normally it grows on the skeletons of gorgonians or on other substrata in favorable positions exposed to the currents. Sometimes it colonizes abandoned nets or the wreckage of sunken ships.

Golden anemone - *Condylactis aurantiaca*

This is a sea anemone typical of sandy or detrital mobile seabeds. It is solitary, with the colony dug into the sediment, and its exposed tentacles open radially. The approximately 100 tentacles are white with lilac-coloured tips. It often hosts symbiotic shrimp from the genus Periclemenes.

Alicia - *Alicia mirabilis*

This is the most beautiful and stinging sea anemone in the Mediterranean. By day it is a mass covered with tubercles, while by night it distends its column and tentacles and can reach a length of one and a half metres. The tubercles are located on the extended column, while the extremely long tentacles are often twisted spiral-fashion and are actively used to capture small prey.

Cladocora - *Cladocora caespitosa*

This is the Mediterranean stony coral most similar to tropical corals. It is a colonial animal, and the form of the colony varies depending on environmental conditions. It most commonly appears as a little cushion with individual corals growing quite close to each other. Usually the only visible part is the end portion of the calcareous skeleton with its cylindrical branches, from which the polyp protrudes with its short, transparent tentacles.

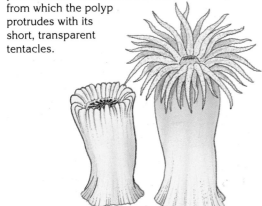

Snakelocks anemone - *Anemonia sulcata*

With about 200 tentacles, this is the largest sea anemone in the Mediterranean. Normally the colony is hidden among the rocks, with only the tentacles visible: they are greenish with violet-lilac tips. It lives in well-illuminated environments, and symbiotic algae are present in its tentacles. Some crustaceans (*Inachus* and *Pilumnus*) and fish (*Gobius bucchichi*) live in contact with the column or among the tentacles.

Parasitic anemone - *Calliactis parasitica*

This is a sea anemone which normally lives in symbiosis with the hermit crab *Dardanus arrosor*. It has a stubby brown column with light vertical stripes. Its tentacles are short and quite numerous (over 500). If disturbed, it issues long, thin, white or lilac-coloured, extremely stinging filaments from the base of the column.

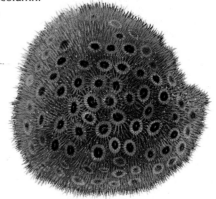

Yellow solitary coral - *Leptosammia pruvoti*

This is a typical stony coral in dimly-illuminated areas, with a hard, lemon yellow skeleton with polyps of the same colour. The tentacles are rough and surround the always visible mouth. This is a solitary species which nevertheless often covers broad areas of the substratum.

Yellow encrusting anemone - *Gerardia savaglia*

This is the false black coral of the Mediterranean, and is only distantly related to true tropical coral. The only black portion is the hard skeleton with the consistency of ebony: the living portion and the polyps are a light yellow colour. It can easily be distinguished from gorgonians due to the large size of its polyps, which clearly extend from the branches.

Bushy anemone - *Parazoanthus axinellae*

Commonly known as the golden zoanthid, this is a colonial animal formed of many individual polyps joined together by a common connective tissue. It is orange yellow in colour and often covers large, poorly illuminated walls fully exposed to the currents. It is easily distinguished from *Leptosammia* by the absence of a skeleton and its smooth tentacles.

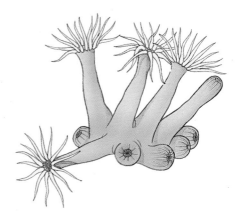

Cylinder anemone - *Cerianthus membranaceus*

Similar to sea anemones, the tube dwelling anemone is nevertheless easily distinguished by its two principal characteristics: it has two groups of tentacles, with the outer ones longer than the inner ones, and a retractile body with a membranous sheath. It has more than 200 tentacles, and their colour varies greatly, from white to dark brown to violet. This animal is typical of areas with a high degree of sedimentation, such as caves or Neptune grass meadows.

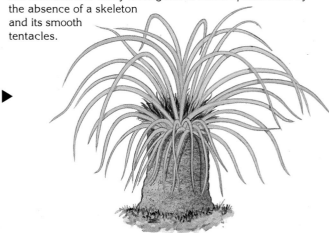

Jewel anemone - *Corynactis viridis*

Although it belongs to another order, the Corallimorpharia, it is quite similar to sea anemones, but does not exceed one centimetre in diameter. It is called the jewel anemone due to its small size and the presence of about a hundred short tentacles that end in a spherical swelling. It can take on quite diverse colours, from lime green to lilac to orange. Usually colonial, it is an animal typical of areas with strong hydrodynamics.

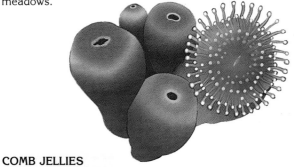

COMB JELLIES

Venus' girdle - *Cestus veneris*

A planktonic animal, the Venus' girdle has a transparent, ribbon-shaped body with rounded extremities. Rows of tiny, continuously vibrating tentacles run across the edge of the body and its middle. The mouth is in the center of the body and receives food captured and transported by the continuous movement of the tentacles. With a body consisting almost entirely of water, it is an extremely fragile animal.

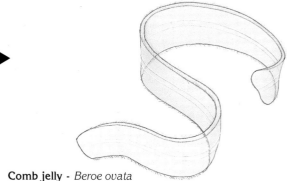

Comb jelly - *Beroe ovata*

The helmet combjelly has a body shaped like a transparent barrel, traversed by several longitudinal rows of vibrating cilia, known as combs, in which the continuous movement of the little tentacles creates a phenomenon of light diffraction. The mouth is in the lower part of the body and receives food carried in along the combs. It can be highly bioluminescent.

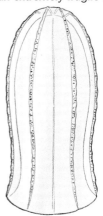

Pink flatworm - *Prosthecaereus giesbrechtii*

This is a platyhelminthe, a very common, brightly coloured flatworm. White and lilac streaks run across its body.
Two small "ears" on the front end serve as sensory organs.
Its mouth is located in the center of the lower portion of the body. It moves by sliding along the seabed using continuously moving cilia located on its underside. It is an active predator of ascidians and mollusks.

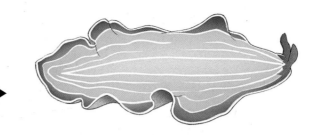

Spiral tube worm - *Sabella spallanzani*

This is the classic spirograph. Its body is protected inside a long tube with a parchment-like texture, from which the large branchial tuft projects. The tuft has respiratory and food gathering functions, and may vary greatly in colour, from dark striped brown to white. The animal is quite sensitive to movement and changes in light, and often retracts.

Red tubicolous worm - *Serpula vermicularis*

This is a spirograph typical of poorly illuminated areas. It has a calcareous tube and a branchial tuft with two pink volutes. A pedunculated operculum is located among the branchiae and is used by the worm to retreat and close the entrance to the tube. It is quite sensitive to the movement of the water that surrounds it and will retract rapidly.

Smooth calcareous worm - *Protula tubularia*

It has a fully visible, calcareous white tube: the bilobate branchial tuft appears more unkempt that those of other spirographs, and usually it is white, although there are red and orange varieties. This animal is quite common in various environments, provided there is adequate sedimentation.

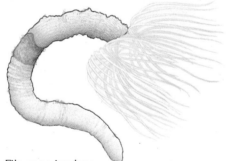

Coral worm - *Filograna implexa*

It looks like a disorderly group of little white tubes that form a rounded mass. It consists of many small individuals with bilobate branchial tufts which are usually transparent, but may be yellow or orange. These annelids live in poorly illuminated environments exposed to currents. They often grow among the branches of gorgonians.

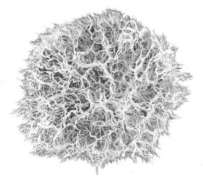

Bonellia - *Bonellia viridis*

It is a member of the Echiuroidea phylum. It has a bean-shaped body with a long proboscis that forks at the end.
It is common in poorly illuminated areas. Sexual dimorphism i s quite accentuated: in fact, the male is quite small and lives as a parasite on the body of the female. The determination of sex is also quite unusual: the larvae become male if they come into contact with a female, while they will develop into females if they fall to the seabed in an area with no females.

MOLLUSKS

Chiton - *Chiton olivaceus*

It has an oval shell composed of 8 jointed pieces, from which the edge of the mantle protrudes. The shell may be many different colours, from olive grey to red to sky blue. It lives under rocks, where it feeds by scraping encrusting algae.

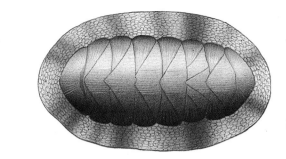

Rayed mediterranean limpet e Ferrous limpet
Patella caerulea and *P. ferruginea*

Limpets have a conical-shaped shell and live at about sea level, attached to the rock by a sturdy foot. They feed on algae which they scrape from the rock with a radula, a sort of toothed tongue. *Patella caerulea* has a flattish shell with no ribbing, while *P. ferruginea* is a larger species that has a high shell with pronounced ribbing. It has become a rare species in Sardinia.

Rough turbo - *Astrea rugosa*

It has a beautiful, spiral-shaped shell with a characteristic operculum used to close the opening. The operculum is orange on the outside, while inside it is light-coloured with a spiral design. Commonly known as the rough turbo, it is used to make pendants. *Astrea rugosa* lives by grazing on algae, and often it is difficult to identify because the shell is covered by a soft layer of algae that can be confused with its surroundings.

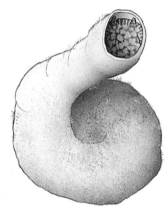

Giant wormshell - *Vermetus arenarius*

It has a tube-shaped shell which assumes a spiral shape only during its developmental stage. Attached to the rocks, this mollusk has a quite unique manner of feeding. It issues a filament of mucous which is carried by the current and attaches to protuberances on the sea floor. The mucous acts as a net that collects suspended organic particles. The filament is withdrawn periodically and the material captured is ingested.

Mediterranean cowrie - *Luria lurida*

This is the most common cowrie in the Mediterranean. Its shell is normally covered by its mantle and remains quite shiny. It is common in dark areas and is nocturnal. It feeds on sponges, which it scrapes with its radula. Considered rare, in reality it is quite common, only difficult to see because it is quite reclusive and mimetic.

Yellow tylodina - *Tylodina perversa*

This is a small sea slug with a cone-shaped shell that does not entirely cover its body. It is bright yellow, with two tentacles on its head, with a large gill on the right side of its body. It feeds exclusively on the sponge *Aplysina aerophoba*, on which it spends most of its life.

Thuridilla - *Thuridilla hopei*

This sea slug is a member of the Sacoglossa order. It has no shell. Its body is elongated, and the upper portion has two lobes which are usually closed. It has two large tentacles on its head. It is quite colourful and feeds on algae, which it grazes primarily in shallow waters.

Giant doris - *Hypselodoris valenciennesi*

This is one of the larger nudibranchs, and some individuals in fact reach a length of 20 centimetres. It has an elongated body with two retractile rhinophores in the front and a branchial tuft which is also retractile on the back portion, which ends in a pointed tail. It can vary greatly in colour, with a light body often marked by azure blue tones covered with yellow streaks and spots.

Dotted sea slug - *Discodoris atromaculata*

This is one of the most common nudibranchs and is quite frequent in Sardinia. It is known as the dotted sea slug due to its characteristic colouring, white with dark spots which are larger in the central portion of its oval-shaped body. Its front portion has two white rhinophores and the branchial tuft. It is a predator specialized in the sponge *Petrosia ficiformis*.

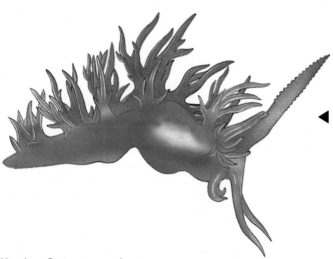

Pink flabellina - *Flabellina affinis*

A quite common nudibranch with a garish violet colour, it lives clinging to colonies of hydrozoans, on which polyps it preys. Its body is covered with elongated appendages traversed by a clear filament which is visible against the light. It may be confused with its relative *Flabellina ischitana*, which is distinguished by the red filaments within its appendages, or with *Coryphella pedata*, which is distinguished by its annular rhinophores.

Hervia - *Cratena peregrina*

This is the most common nudibranch in Sardinia, and can be seen during almost every dive. It has a white body covered with long orange-violet appendages. Its front portion has two clear orange spots between the white oral tentacles and orange rhinophores. It feeds on hydrozoans, on which colonies it also lays its eggs with their tangled white filaments.

Noble pen shell - *Pinna nobilis*

This is the largest bivalve in the Mediterranean, and mature specimens about 20 years old can reach one metre in length. It lives in detrital environments and Neptune grass meadows, where it is often colonized by other organisms such as sponges, hydrozoans and ascidians. It hosts symbiotic shrimp and crabs. It is a highly protected species and is increasingly rare along the coast of Sardinia.

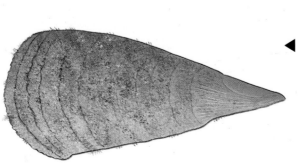

Winged shell - *Pteria hirundo*

Its shell is wing-shaped, and it normally lives in environments exposed to currents. It often lives on colonies of sea fans or other gorgonians, taking advantage of the favorable position. This bivalve clings to the branches of its host by means of a byssus, a group of sturdy filaments which solidify upon contact with water.

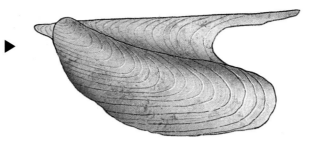

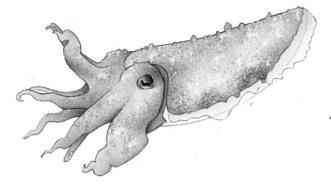

Common cuttlefish - *Sepia officinalis*

This is a cephalopod which retains a residual shell: the cuttlebone. It has eight short tentacles and two longer ones which are used to capture its prey. The cuttlefish is quite mimetic and can rapidly change colour. Its eggs are round with a pointed bottom, and hatch into fully formed little cuttlefish.

Common octopus - *Octopus vulgaris*

The octopus is a cephalopod with eight arms, and is capable of camouflaging itself by changing both the colour and form of its body. It is an extremely intelligent animal, and laboratory experiments have shown that it is capable of learning by observing others. After mating, the female lays her eggs in a cavity and guards them without eating until they hatch: for this reason females often die after reproduction.

White spotted octopus - *Octopus macropus*

Known as the white spotted octopus, it has longer tentacles than the common octopus and is almost exclusively nocturnal. It can easily be distinguished by its reddish brown colour with quite visible white spots over its entire body. Like the common octopus, it lives in all environments down to depths of about 100 metres.

CRUSTACEANS

Barnacle - *Balanus perforatus*

This is commonly known as the acorn barnacle. It lives within a conical shell firmly anchored to the rocks or artificial substrata, with its upper portion closed by four mobile plates. Within its shell, the animal lives lying on its "back," and feeds by capturing suspended particles through its cirri, modified claws, which are continuously extended and retracted in and out of the shell.

Mediterranean cleaner shrimp - *Stenopus spinosus*

Known as the banded shrimp, it lives exclusively in dark caves. Its body is orange yellow and its third pair of claws, which are quite long, end in pincers. The long white antennae on its head are used to communicate with its "customers," the large fish such as groupers and amberjacks which it cleans.

Narval shrimp - *Pesionika narval*

This shrimp can be found in dark caves, where it lives in groups of dozens of individuals. It has an extremely long, toothed front rostrum, long white antennae and an elongated body streaked with red and white. It is commonly found on sandy seabeds down to great depths, even beyond 800 metres.

▶

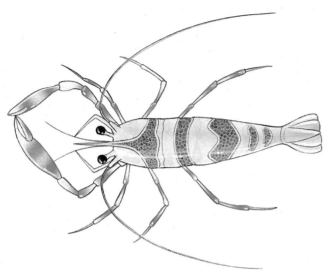

Periclimenes - *Periclemenes amethysteus*

◀ This is also known as the anemone shrimp. It has an almost completely transparent body with some pink-coloured areas. It often lives in symbiosis with the sea anemones *Codylactis aurantiaca* and *Cribrinopsis crassa*. There are other similar species, such as *P. sagittifer*, which has violet spots and a pronounced V-shaped mark on the abdomen.

Lobster - *Homarus gammarus*

Unlike the spiny lobster, this lobster has two large asymmetrical claws. It is a deep yellow colour with blue spots, while its antennae are red. It lives in caves and cavities, from which it comes out at night to hunt. It can become quite large, and is usually sedentary and territorial.

▶

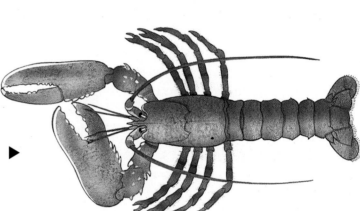

Common spiny lobster - *Palinurus elephas*

The spiny lobster lives on rocky seabeds in coralligenous areas, but can also be found in rocky areas among meadows of Neptune grass. It has long antennae with a sensory function, no claws, and it generally feeds on dead animals. It is commonly ◀ fished.

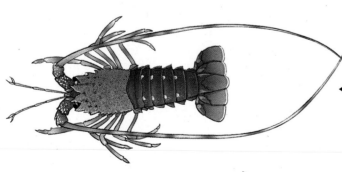

Mediterranean locust lobster - *Scyllarides latus*

The squill or locust lobster is common in dark areas. Its antennae are modified into two wide, jointed plates. A large red spot similar to an eye can be seen on its abdomen, directly behind its shell. In late spring it comes to the surface to deposit its eggs. It is considered an increasingly rare species and is in any event localized. The small locust lobster (*Scyllarus arctus*) is a similar but smaller species.

▶

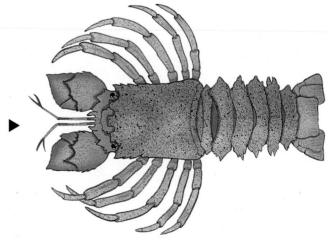

Ridged claw hermit crab - *Dardanus arrosor*

This is the classic hermit crab, bright red with two sturdy claws.
Like all hermit crabs, it has a soft abdomen which it protects
within shells or other suitable containers. Usually a number of
sea anemones (*Calliactis parasitica*) can be found on its shell,
with which it lives symbiotically. The sea anemones protect
the hermit crab, while the anemones enjoy better feeding
opportunities.

▶

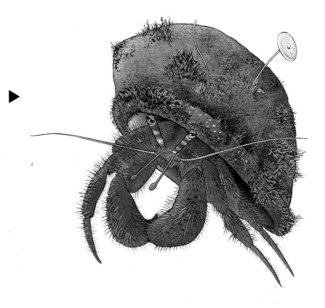

Spiny squat-lobster - *Galathea strigosa*

Although it does not have a soft abdomen, it belongs to the
same group as the hermit crabs. It is a beautiful red-orange
colour with azure blue streaks, and lives exclusively in dark
cracks, from which it comes out at night to hunt. It has two
well-developed pincers and long antennae on its head.
It moves quite quickly in sudden jerks.

◀

Sleepy crab - *Dromia personata*

This is also known as the porter crab because, especially when
young, it breaks off a piece of sponge from the wall and uses it
to cover itself, carrying it along constantly and holding it above
its body with its two claws. This crab has a rounded carapace
and two sturdy pincers which are a delicate pink colour.

▶

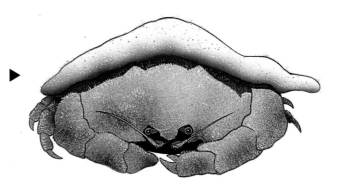

Spiny spider crab - *Maja squinado*

The spinous spider crab has a convex, oval-shaped carapace
with a spiny edge. It is a yellow brown colour and has long,
lighter-coloured appendages. It is nocturnal, and during the
mating season forms large groups near the surface. A similar
but smaller species, *Maja verrucosa*, has a carapace covered
with algae, sponges and hydrozoans that make it difficult to
spot.

◀

BRYOZOANS

False coral - *Myriapora truncata*

It has a branched, erect orange skeleton covered by fine hairs. The colony is comprised of the tentacles of individual specimens located within little holes along the entire skeleton. It is an orange-red colour and is known as false coral. Although it is often confused with coral, the presence of the holes on its skeleton makes it easy to identify. It is common in poorly illuminated areas.

▶

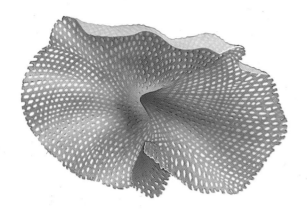

Neptunes' lace- *Sertella septentrionalis*

◀ This is known as sea lace bryozoan. It grows in finely perforated laminae in the form of a cup with fluted edges. Pinkish in colour, it lives in poorly illuminated areas, and despite its hardness, it is quite fragile.

ECHINODERMS

Featherstar - *Antedon mediterranea*

This is commonly known as the crinoid. It has a small, button-shaped body with about ten flexible arms with a group of pinnules on each side. On the other side of its body it has a group of cirri that permit it to grasp onto the substratum. It feeds on suspended particles, which it collects with its arms and brings to its mouth, located in the center of the body and turned upwards, through the movement of small bristles.

▶

Cotton spinner - *Holothuria tubulosa*

◀ The sea cucumber has a tube-shaped body with a mouth at the front end and an anus at the other. The upper portion of the body is scattered with small conical protuberances, while the lower side is traversed by pedicles that permit it to move. It feeds on detritus by swallowing and sifting sediment.

Purple sea star - *Ophidiaster ophidianus*

This is a large red star, with arms that often exceed 20 centimetres in length. The surface of its body appears velvety, and its colour varies from dark red to orange spotted with red. The lower side of the body is lighter, and ambulatory pedicles extend from furrows along the arms.

▶

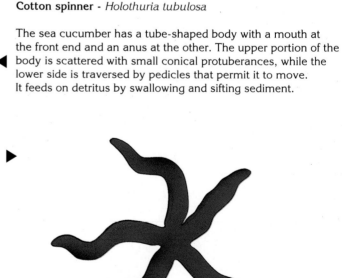

Red starfish - *Echinaster sepositus*

◀ The is the most common red star. It has a rough body with five arms, sometimes more, which are cylindrical and furrowed on the lower side, from which the pedicles protrude. It feeds on other invertebrates and is common in all environments to over 200 metres deep.

Mediterranean longspined urchin - *Centrostephanus longispinus*

The long-spined urchin is difficult to spot, not because it is rare, but because it is quite reclusive, with nocturnal habits. It lives in dark areas where it inserts itself into cracks with its long tentacles. The upper part of its body has small reddish-purple spines which are in continuous movement.

▶

Black sea urchin - *Arbacia lixula*

◀ Totally black in colour, this species is commonly known as the black sea urchin. It grazes on algae in well-illuminated areas, scraping encrusting red algae from the rocks and often grazing the rocks bare.

Violet sea urchin - *Sphaerechinus granularis*

This is known as the whitetip sea urchin. Many specimens have white-tipped spines, while some are totally white. It is almost spherical in form and is common on meadows of Neptune grass, on which rhizomes and roots it feeds.

▶

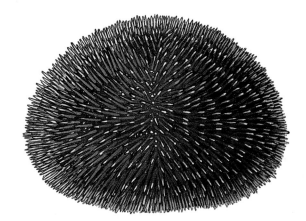

Stony seaurchin - *Paracentrotus lividus*

This is known as the stony sea urchin. Its colour may vary from brown, green to dark violet-blue, and it is common in well illuminated areas, where it grazes on algae with soft thalli. ◀ As it does not like the light, however, it covers its body with fragments of algae and other objects, and is thus easily distinguishable from *Arbacia lixula*.

Purple heart urchin - *Spatangus purpureus*

This is a heart urchin which by day lives buried in the sediment. Its exoskeleton has an ovoid, heart-shaped form covered with a fine pale purple fuzz, from which grow a few longer, thin spines. Like all heart urchins, it feeds by gathering edible matter from the sediment, separating it from inorganic matter.

▶

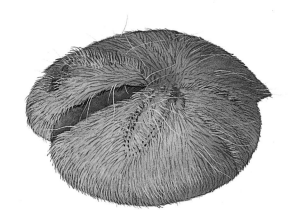

TUNICATES

Light bulb sea squirt - *Clavelina lepadiformis*

This is a colonial ascidian. The colony is formed by various individuals joined by a common stolon at the base. Each individual is connected to the stolon by a peduncle, surmounted by a transparent body with two characteristic orifices. It is quite common on rocky seabeds in late spring, and can form large groups. It feeds by filtering organic material.

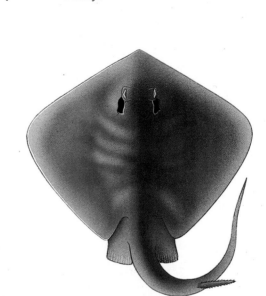

Red sea squirt - *Halocinthya papillosa*

This is a solitary ascidian with a characteristic bright red colour. Also known as the sea potato, it has a thick, rough tunic and is quite sensitive to light and movement, withdrawing rapidly. It is very common in all environments with dim light. It reproduces sexually.

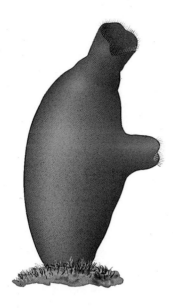

FISH

Common stingray - *Dasyatis pastinaca*

This is a cartilaginous fish with a characteristic rhomboidal form with a long, tapered tail with a serrated spine used as a defensive weapon. Known as the stingray, it lives on the sea floor, often covered with sediment from detrital or sandy seabeds. It feeds on various creatures, and captures fish, crustaceans and mollusks.

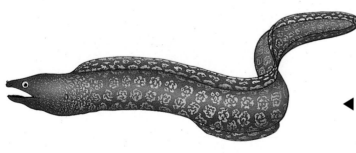

Mediterranean moray - *Murena helena*

One of the most common fish, the moray is wrongly considered ferocious and dangerous. It lives in crevices from which only the front portion of its body protrudes. It comes out to hunt only at night and feeds primarily on octopuses, but also on fish and crustaceans. Its mouth is always wide open, showing its teeth, in order to oxygenate its gills.

Conger eel - *Conger conger*

The conger eel has a tapered body which is a uniform grey colour, and it may reach quite large dimensions. By day it lives hidden in crevices among the rocks, and it is quite common around sunken ships. By night it comes out of its lair to hunt, feeding primarily on fish. One of its principal reproduction areas is the very deep waters to the southeast of Sardinia.

Forkbeard - *Phycis phycis*

The forkbeard is common in dark areas. It is a member of the cod family and can easily be distinguished by the two barbels below the mouth and its ventral fins in the form of a forked filament, which has a tactile function. It has two dorsal fins; the second dorsal fin and the anal fin are symmetrical and extend to the tail.

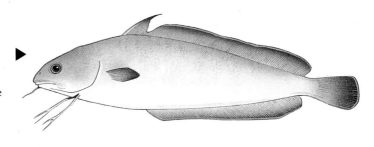

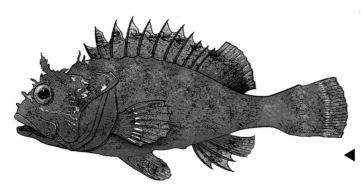

John dory - *Zeus faber*

The John Dory has an unmistakable appearance: its body, compressed at the sides, is oval and surmounted by the extremely long rays of the dorsal fin. Its ventral and anal fins are also quite generous. It has a very large mouth which is turned upward and can be extroverted. It is a yellowish silvery colour with a large dark spot in the form of an ocellus. According to legend, the spot is the mark left by the hand of St. Peter.

Sea horse - *Hippocampus guttulatus*

The easily recognizable seahorse usually lives with its tail gripping algae, invertebrates or leaves of Neptune grass. It swims slowly in an erect position, frenetically agitating its transparent dorsal fin. The male incubates and hatches the eggs in a ventral sac. It always appears unkempt and sad.

Red Scorpionfish - *Scorpaena scrofa*

The red scorpionfish is characterized by a large head followed by two broad pectoral fins and a stubby body. Its head is full of leaf-shaped protuberances, which along with its colour increase the general mimetic effect. The spines of its dorsal fin and the operculum can emit a powerful poison which can cause intense pain. The poison is thermolabile, and immersion of the injured part into warm water relieves the pain.

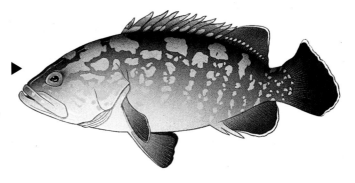

Dusky grouper - *Epinephelus marginatus*

The grouper can become quite large. Its body is often very broad, and although it rarely exceeds a metre in length, it can weigh more than 50 kilograms. It often hovers vertically, slowly moving its wide pectoral fins. It takes shelter in deep, complex lairs. Younger individuals are female, while after sexual inversion older specimens become male.

Comber - *Serranus cabrilla*

The comber is quite common in all environments. It has a prominent mandible and a brown-striped body. It is a hermaphrodite species, possessing both male and female gonads which are active at the same time. It has not yet been determined whether it is self-fertilizing.

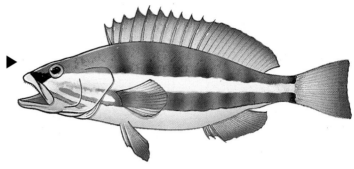

Painted comber - *Serranus scriba*

The painted comber or sea perch is brightly coloured. Its head is streaked with a network of red and blue lines, and its back has dark stripes alternating with yellow. It has a very evident light blue spot on its stomach. It often follows the movements of octopuses and is thus an indicator of their presence. It is hermaphroditic and feeds on small fish and crustaceans.

European seabass - *Dicentrarchus labrax*

The sea bass is a swift predator with an elongated, silvery body. It can become quite large, up to a metre in length. Reproduction takes place in winter, when groups of males fertilize the eggs of a single female. The sea bass adapts well to brackish waters as well, and thus is easy to breed.

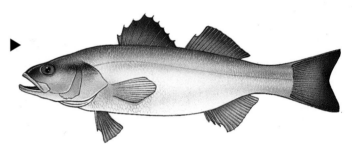

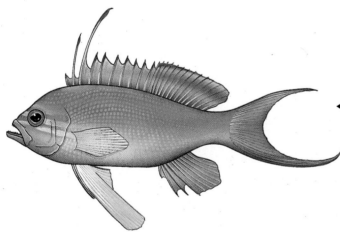

Swallowtail seaperch - *Anthias anthias*

The swallowtail sea perch lives in large schools on deep reefs and in coralligenous areas. As it increases in size it changes sex from female to male. Usually it forms groups of females with a single dominant male. The species exhibits clear sexual dimorphism, with males being more brightly coloured with longer fins.

Cardinal fish - *Apogon imberbis*

The cardinal fish is a small red fish with large dark eyes striped with white. It lives in sizable groups in dark areas, in caves and under rocky masses. Reproduction takes place by means of a sort of coupling in which the eggs are fecundated by means of the fins. The male then collects the fertilized eggs and watches over them until they hatch about 8 days later.

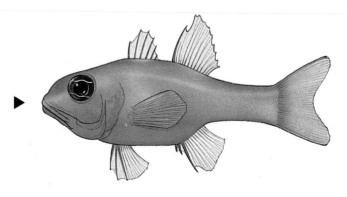

Greater amberjack - *Seriola dumerilli*

The amberjack is a sizable pelagic predator which lives in large schools. It exhibits the homochromy typical of pelagic fish: the upper portion of its body is dark, while the lower portion is light. A dark streak runs diagonally across its head. Young individuals are a bright yellow-gold colour.

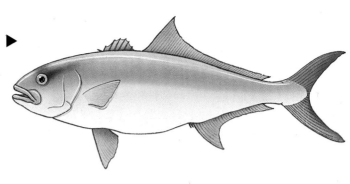

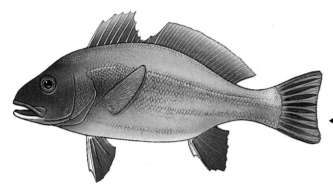

Brown meagre - *Sciaena umbra*

The brown meagre is a common fish in dark areas: it lives in small groups in caves among rocky masses. It has a characteristic brownish bronze colour and the edges of its fins are gold. The first dorsal fin is quite elongated. It can make sounds which are often quite audible underwater.

Striped red mullet - *Mullus surmuletus*

The striped red mullet is easily recognizable by the brick red band that runs the length of its body and the two barbels under its mouth. The two appendages have a sensory function and are utilized to identify the small invertebrates on which it feeds.

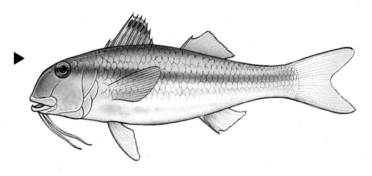

Black seabream - *Spondyliosoma cantharus*

The black seabream is a member of the Sparidae family. It has an oval, compressed body. It usually lives in large groups which can be found in all environments. It is a sequentially hermaphroditic species: it is female when young, while adults are male. It reproduces in the spring, depositing its eggs in sandy areas.

Annular seabream - *Diplodus annularis*

The annular bream is the smallest of this genus, and can be distinguished from the others by its yellowish colour and its elongated oval form. It appears to be a protandrous hermaphrodite: first male and then female. It is common in all environments at shallow depths.

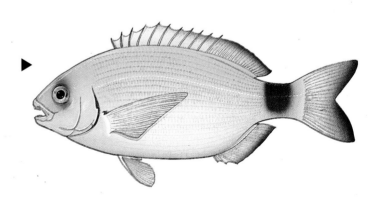

163

White seabream - *Diplodus sargus*

The white seabream has an oval, silvery body with a black spot on the caudal peduncle. It can reach 50 centimetres in length and has quite large teeth which are capable of crushing the skeleton of sea urchins. It has separate sexes and lives primarily in rocky environments.

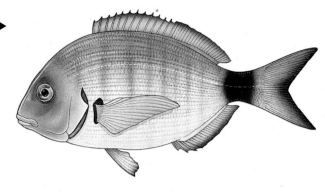

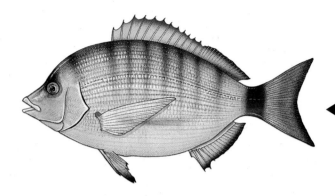

Sharpsnout seabream - *Diplodus puntazzo*

The sharpsnout seabream can easily be distinguished by its pointed snout, its dark vertical stripes, more or less visible, and the dark spot on its caudal peduncle. It is the least sedentary of the seabreams and feeds on both invertebrates and algae.

Common twobanded seabream - *Diplodus vulgaris*

The two-banded seabream is characterized by two black bands on the back of its head and on the caudal peduncle. It can become just as big as the two larger species, but normally it is found in sizable schools of smaller individuals. It is a hermaphroditic species, but there is no precise pattern to its sexual phases.

Common dentex - *Dentex dentex*

The dentex is a large pelagic predator which lives in schools near deep reefs. It is silvery with violet blue tones and small turquoise spots. It can become quite large, and the biggest individuals are usually solitary. During the night it often rests on the seabed to sleep, sometimes within caves. It has very large teeth.

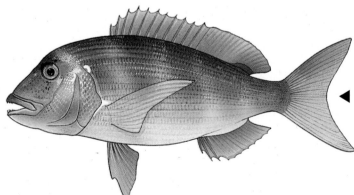

Saddled seabream - *Oblada melanura*

The saddled seabream is silvery with a black spot edged in white located on the caudal peduncle. Its body is elongated and its mouth is turned slightly upwards. It moves in large groups that often hover just a few metres below the surface. It feeds on animals and plants on the seabed and near the surface.

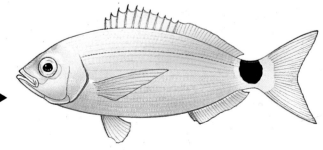

Salema - *Sarpa salpa*

The salema is a classical gregarious fish which is easily distinguished by the golden yellow horizontal stripes that run across it. It has a small mouth which it uses to graze on algae on the seabed or on leaves of Neptune grass. It is a sequential hermaphrodite: first male and then female.

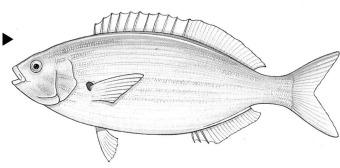

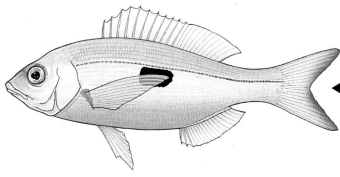

Blotched picarel - *Spicara maena*

The blotched pickerel is a small gregarious fish which normally lives in large schools just a few metres from the surface. It has an elongated body with a black spot in the middle of both sides. It is a sequentially hermaphroditic species: first female and then male. During the reproduction period males become brightly coloured, with azure blue stripes and spots.

Damselfish - *Chromis chromis*

The damselfish is extremely common and can be seen during any dive, in large schools that hover near the surface of the water. Reproduction takes place on the sea floor, where the females deposit the eggs in an area cleaned by the male, who then watches over them until they hatch. Young individuals have an unmistakable electric blue colour.

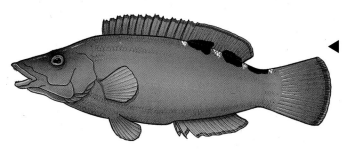

Cockoo wrasse - *Labrus bimaculatus*

This is one of the most colourful wrasses, with an accentuated sexual dimorphism. Females are a light purple-red colour with black and white spots under the dorsal fin. Males are orange with azure stripes over their entire bodies and tails with azure blue edges. It is a sequential hermaphrodite: first female and then male.

Peacock wrasse - *Symphodus tinca*

The peacock wrasse exhibits evident sexual dimorphism. The smaller females are less colourful, while males have a green and blue snout with dark blue stripes, a yellow body with horizontal blue stripes spotted with red and azure fins with turquoise spots. It is a protandrous hermaphrodite.

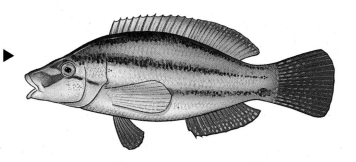

Axillary wrasse - *Symphodus mediterraneus*

The axillary wrasse exhibits sexual differentiation from birth.
The sexual dimorphism becomes more accentuated during
the reproductive period, when males take on a brick red colour
with a noticeably yellow eye and a yellow spot at the base
of the pectoral fins. The male builds the nest with algae and
detritus and the female deposits her eggs within it.

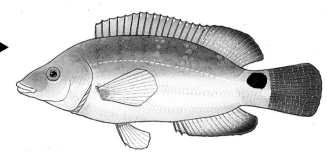

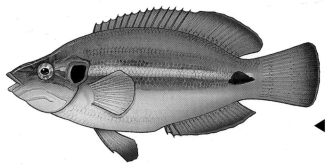

Ocellated wrasse - *Symphodus ocellatus*

The ocellated wrasse takes its name from a characteristic spot
behind the eye, green edged with red and azure blue. The male
is more colourful than the female, with green and orange stripes
on its head and fins. The male uses algae to build a nest, where
it watches over the eggs deposited there by the female.

Rainbow wrasse - *Coris julis*

The rainbow wrasse exhibits clear sexual differentiation and is
a protogynous hermaphrodite. Females are smaller than males
and are a brick red colour on their upper backs with one white
and one yellow stripe along their sides. The larger males have
a gaudy orange stripe along their sides, with the stomach white
in front and green near the tail. Rainbow wrasses are voracious
predators and feed on invertebrates.

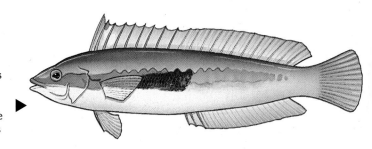

Ornate wrasse - *Thalassoma pavo*

The ornate wrasse is the most "tropical" of the Mediterranean
fish due to the three different colour combinations it can
assume. A sequential hermaphrodite, its colour varies as it
transforms from female to male, with a transition colour as
well. The males are the most colourful, with a turquoise head
with red stripes, yellow, red and turquoise bands and a red
stripe behind the head. The rest of the body is green, with blue
fins. It feeds on invertebrates.

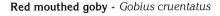

Red mouthed goby - *Gobius cruentatus*

The red-mouthed goby has an elongated body, and like all
gobies lives on the seabed. It has two characteristic red spots
on its mouth, and a body with brown and white spots.
The two dorsal fins are elongated, while the ventral fins form
the adhesive disc characteristic of gobies. It feeds primarily
on invertebrates.

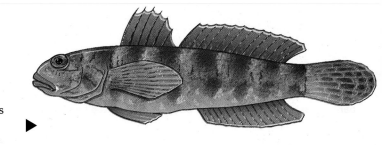

Slender goby - *Gobius geniporus*

It has the distinctive form of all gobies, with a light-coloured body with dark spots. Its eyes are emerald green. When it lives on the sand or detritus it is quite mimetic and easy to approach. It feeds on invertebrates.

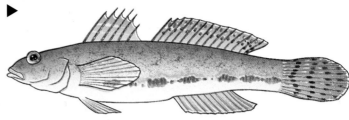

Tompot blenny - *Parablennius gattorugine*

The tompot blenny has a large head with bulging red eyes surmounted by fringed tentacles. The long dorsal fin runs across its elongated body, which has vertical reddish stripes. The two pectoral fins are quite broad and are always spread. It is a territorial species, especially during the reproductive period, when males attempt to have a number of females deposit their eggs in the lair they have selected.

Long striped blenny - *Parablennius rouxi*

This is a small blenny with a white body with a longitudinal dark brown stripe. It has small feathery tentacles on its head. It often lives within holes in the rock or the empty tubes of spirographs, from which only its head protrudes with its two large eyes. It is commonly known as the striped blenny.

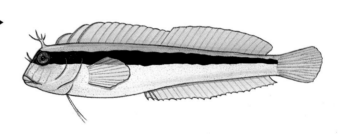

Red blackfaced blenny - *Trypterigion tripteronotus*

The black-faced blenny is a small fish that always lives in contact with the seabed. It has an elongated body with a pointed head. During the reproductive period males are quite colourful, with bright red bodies and black heads; they perform complicated courting rituals to attract females. It feeds on invertebrates.

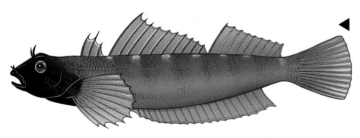

European barracuda - *Sphyraena sphyraena*

This barracuda belongs to the same family as the tropical barracudas. It has an elongated body with a pointed head and a prominent jaw with pointed teeth. It can become quite large, but usually it is seen in schools of dozens of medium-sized individuals. It is a swift predator and feeds on fish, mollusks and crustaceans.

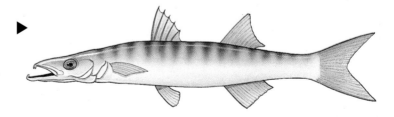

EPILOGUE: A BOOK OF DREAMS FOR PROTECTED AREAS

168 A group of dolphins (Tursiops truncatus) swims near the island of Tavolara on a day when the water is calm. The elusive bottle-nose dolphins are the most common cetaceans along the Sardinian coast.

*Cover
At Su Puntillone reef two spirographs (Sabella spallanzani), with their unusual white tuft, stand out among the damselfish.*

*Back cover - top
Off the coast of Tavolara, the wall of Secca del Papa is covered with gaudy, rare red and yellow gorgonian sea fans (Paramuricea clavata).*

*Back cover - bottom
The lilac-colored expanse of jewel anemones (Corinactis viridis) on the vertical rocks of Su Puntillone reef is one of the hidden pearls of the sea of Sardinia.*

Writing a guide to scuba diving in Sardinia necessarily leads to a paradox: the most popular diving area for many enthusiasts who choose Sardinia for their diving is in France - in Corsica, to be exact! During the summer months, dozens of boats and hundreds of divers crowd Lavezzi Reef (now known as "grouper reef") every day, coming from a broad stretch of the Sardinian coast from Porto Rotundo to beyond Santa Teresa di Gallura. The island of Lavezzi, just a few miles from the islands of the La Maddalena archipelago, has for many years been a protected area, where constant and attentive control, gentle but well-aimed restrictions and a favorable environment have created an underwater situation that only three or four other areas in the Mediterranean can offer. The only difference between Lavezzi Reef and Sardinia is the far-sightedness of those involved in environmental protection in Corsica and France.

But now a new season has begun in Sardinia as well: the dream of opening the national parks of La Maddalena, the Gulf of Orosei and Asinara, as well as the marine reserves of Capo Caccia, Tavolara, Sinis and Capo Carbonara, has become a reality, and marine parks have actually been created where scuba diving and its related tourism will be natural developments.

It is hoped that this book will make a small, concrete contribution of knowledge that will encourage the development of a network of protected marine areas and a tourist industry compatible with the use and conservation of the extraordinary marine environments that surround the island.